D0066126

It is possible to love your spouse, your kids, and your work. I know because I have somehow managed to pull it off. But I can tell you it doesn't happen accidentally. It is definitely intentional. My wonderful wife and I picked the brains of everyone we admired for their relationships.

André and Jeff have done the same thing in creating this book. In fact, they are kind of obsessed about it. Whether over dinners or during podcasts, they have examined the lives of couples who love each other and what they do. Their research is thoughtful, thorough, and often humorously candid. But most of all, it is extremely valuable.

Loving your family and your work results in a rich, rewarding life, and who doesn't want that? This book can set you on that path. Enjoy!

JEFF FOXWORTHY, comedian

There is so much we could say about these two, but I think letting you know up front that they're the friends you never realized you were missing is a good start. André and Jeff are two of the most grounded, intelligent, authentic, and hopeful people we know. Rarely does the world get to see a duo like this, who explicitly live out their values—in their partnership, parenting, and careers. We are a better couple simply for knowing and loving them.

JULIET AND KYLE KORVER, artist and NBA All-Star

In *Love or Work*, André and Jeff Shinabarger provide helpful and hopeful language for many of the questions and challenges we face as we navigate relationships and life as a whole. It is a field guide providing practical insight, lined with grace, giving the reader tools to journey onward into deeper connection at a mindful and intentional pace.

MORGAN HARPER NICHOLS, artist and poet

This book addresses a tension that everyone feels but not many people talk about. It's given us language to be more intentional about what kind of life we are creating and why. This should be required reading for adults.

ANDY AND CRISTINA MINEO, hip-hop artist and entrepreneur

Combining purpose and family is a never-ending tension. This book is a must-read for the journey.

SCOTT HARRISON, *New York Times* bestselling author of *Thirst*

As a couple who started two businesses within our first year of marriage, we truly resonate with this book. Jeff and André have done the hard work for you, compiling wisdom that's priceless for learning how to balance love and work and everything in between. With unique interactive elements to create dialogue with your partner, this is a must-read for any couple wanting to build a legacy that lasts.

SARAH DUBBELDAM, founder and CEO of Darling Media
STEVE DUBBELDAM, founder and CEO of Wilderness Collective

As an ambitious entrepreneur, I've long feared that I couldn't cultivate a loving partnership, raise an amazing family, *and* create the business of my dreams. *Love or Work* shows you that you don't have to choose. It is possible—and it's within reach.

AMBER RAE, bestselling author of *Choose Wonder Over Worry*

We're (thankfully) entering into a new moment in culture where the belief that our roles in marriage have less to do with a centuries-old script based on our gender alone and more to do with who we are uniquely made to be (our gifts, passion, and vision) and how those things intersect (or, let's be honest, occasionally conflict) with our forever partner. While this brave new world has many merits, it also comes with a new set of challenges. And this book is the road map we need. André and Jeff have given us an incredible gift: the (sometimes painfully) honest truth of their own story married with insights on broad cultural trends and the stories of other couples navigating modern love and work. All of it is lighting the way, inspiring and challenging us to do the hard and life-giving work of building lives of deep purpose *and* committed, forever love. André and Jeff are bolstering our belief that it is indeed possible to love and work and most importantly reminding us that we are not alone as we fumble and flail a bit along the way.

LIZ FORKIN BOHANNON, cofounder of Sseko Designs, author of *Beginner's Pluck*

# LOVE or WORK

IS IT POSSIBLE TO CHANGE THE WORLD, STAY IN LOVE & RAISE A HEALTHY FAMILY?

# LOVE or WORK

ANDRÉ & JEFF SHINABARGER

ZONDERVAN THRIVE

*Love or Work*


Requests for information should be addressed to:
Zondervan, *3900 Sparks Dr. SE, Grand Rapids, Michigan 49546*

Zondervan titles may be purchased in bulk for educational, business, fundraising, or sales promotional use. For information, please email SpecialMarkets@Zondervan.com.

ISBN 978-0-310-35830-5 (hardcover)
ISBN 978-0-310-35832-9 (audio)
ISBN 978-0-310-35831-2 (ebook)



The authors are represented by The Christopher Ferebee Agency, www.christopherferebee.com.

Zondervan Thrive, an imprint of Zondervan, publishes books that empower readers with insightful, expert-driven ideas for a life of thriving in today's world.

*Cover design: Tim Green / Faceout Studio*
*Cover type illustrations: Michaella Till, Yellow Bird Visuals*
*Author photo: Mary Claire Stewart*
*Interior design: Denise Froehlich*
*Interior designed quotes: Alexandra Nelson, @alimakesthings*

*Printed in the United States of America*

---

20 21 22 23 24 /LSC/ 10 9 8 7 6 5 4 3 2 1

*To Jada and Neko*

*May the words in this book*
*be the story of our family*
*and your future families.*

*We love you.*

# *Contents*

# *Foreword*

In 2016 I was stressed out. I was writing and recording an album, navigating the chaos of young children—four, seven, and eight years old—and wondering why my marriage was suffering. Our date nights were full of silence, unless we were processing how to deal with our children. Our connectionless convos were interrupted by emails and texts I felt obligated to respond to. I remember sitting across from my wife, realizing we were at this restaurant out of sheer obligation. This is what good married couples do. They go on dates. Aren't dates supposed to be about connecting? We definitely were *not* doing that. It would take some time before we hit rock bottom and made intentional strides toward restoration. I thought I could balance it all. I thought if I just stayed up a little later, woke up a little earlier, and worked a little harder, I'd arrive at perfect peace and harmony.

Many people spend great portions of their lives searching for balance. This great treasure sought after from generation to generation always appears attainable, yet it seems no one has unearthed it. At the bottom of my emails, my signature is "Busyness and productivity are not the same." I write that as a reminder to myself. I am a husband, father of three, touring musician, author, film producer, actor, and entrepreneur. I'm always busy. But am I always productive? I had a burning desire to trade the juggling act for balance. But I never found it. What I did find in the process was something incredibly beautiful. I found healthy tension.

You see, balance assumes there is a utopian lifestyle that manages to give just the right amount of time to your marriage, your faith, your children, yourself, and your work. Balance assumes there will be no variables. But tragedies, transitions, losses, and changes create a roller coaster in our lives. How can we possibly prepare for these things, let alone find perfect balance?

Balance is an ideal. It's a fairy tale found in movies. It's not art imitating life. It's art reimagining life. That in itself isn't a bad thing until it becomes an ultimate thing. We find ourselves chasing gold at the end of the rainbow instead of celebrating the beauty of the rainbow itself. I think healthy tension *is* the rainbow. The tension of keeping all the balls in the air, spending quality time with your children, celebrating love with your spouse, and working to provide versus working within your passion—this is where beauty is found.

I learned that none of it will ever be done perfectly, but all of it can be done intentionally. Small steps led to great gains. I left my phone off for the first few hours after coming home. I came up with a list of questions to ask each other on date nights. I declined those meetings "that will change everything" and opted to ride a bike with my kids. I learned that the world would go on fine without me. I also learned that embracing my imperfections and giving myself the grace to drop a ball here or there was incredibly powerful. It's easier to pick up a dropped ball and keep juggling when you know you've dropped it somewhere along the line.

What you should grasp from this book is that life isn't about having it all together (or worse, pretending you have it all together); it's about constantly admitting you don't. You can't work on problems that you don't acknowledge. I have never found perfect balance, but I have found healthy tension. I don't run from it; I run toward it. The process makes me better. I wasn't created to do it all; I was created to experience the freedom of clarity. Sometimes the joy is in the journey, not the destination.

I have known Jeff and André for many years and have watched them honestly wrestle with the same daily tensions as I do. They don't have all the answers; none of us do. They may have reached different conclusions than your family does. But I know and believe their journey will help your journey.

LECRAE

# Introduction

Warning. You are about to read a book that will disrupt your life. This is not your typical book. It is a book about work, relationships, and parenting. You should read this if you are in a relationship (or not), you should read this if you have kids (or are even just thinking about having kids), and you should read this if you work (or are passionate about good work in the world). But most of all you should read this if you feel the strain between love and work. We hope this book disrupts your life by instigating conversations with your partner that have needed to happen . . . but haven't.

This book is our story. We've never found a marriage book to help us navigate these tension-filled waters. (Also, the majority of marriage books we read are written by men—which is a problem.) That's why we wrote this book *together.* We believe you need to hear *both* perspectives. We both love our work. We both love each other. We also both love our crazy little humans who belong to us. The intersection of all three of these loves creates big stressors in our relationships, doesn't it? This strain between love and work has been the core struggle throughout our relationship. Maybe you feel this tension too?

You might be in the messy middle of some of these hard questions:

- Do I have to stop working once we have kids?

- Whose job is more important?
- When do I find time to go out with a friend, work out, or even read a book?
- My father (or mother) was a workaholic; how do I balance my time between work and family?
- I'm so exhausted by the end of the day. Who has time for sex?

In the midst of trying to answer these unresolved questions ourselves, people started asking us for advice. Our lack of responses led to this book. We were wrestling with the same things. We know of many stories that included divorce, resentment, and burnout. But we hoped there could be another way. We needed to find couples proverbially planting stories of hope and possibility. We wanted to find the people doing it all. What was their secret? How did they juggle family and work and still grow their love for fifty years together?

We did what we know how to do best: we bombarded them with questions. We asked friends, CEOs, couples working together, couples in second marriages, couples together for forty years, and newlyweds. We stayed curious. We hosted dinners and peeled back layers upon layers of tensions surrounding marriage. Our hearts filled with so much encouragement that we had to bring more people to the table: *you*. We wanted people to hear these amazing conversations, so we went on an adventure. We jumped into an Airstream and traveled the country to find more couples, ask more questions, and record more interviews (more about that crazy escapade later in the book).

And that, friends, is how *Love or Work* began.

Since that day, we have interviewed one hundred couples (check out our podcast *Love or Work*) and partnered with Barna Research to survey 1,501 working people about this topic. Now we get to share our findings with you.

Throughout this book we take turns writing chapters. We want you to feel part of our story.

As this book came to fruition, we came to an epiphany:

1. Both of our names are on the cover of this book, and
2. neither of us agrees 100 percent with everything the other has written, and
3. there is a possibility you won't agree with us either.
4. That's okay.

So, welcome to our life and welcome to our marriage. We disagree . . . a lot. We hope showing our contrasting views at times makes you feel more comfortable and our story more relatable. We want you to feel like you could be sitting at a table having this conversation with us. We want you to laugh at our crazy stories, know you are not alone in your struggles, and feel inspired to pursue work, family, love, and dialogue with your partner.

Most chapters include honest conversations between the two of us, stories from our interviews, statistics gleaned from our research, a challenge for you to do together, and a *Love or Work* podcast episode that relates to the chapter. Also, at the end of each chapter, we provide questions for you to answer individually and/or with your partner. These questions have been carefully curated to stimulate conversation with your love. This book is not meant to be prescriptive (although you may find some helpful tips along the way), but we hope it inspires you to live your dreams and have a healthy, joy-filled family.

Is it possible to change the world, stay in love, and raise a healthy family?

We hope so.

André and Jeff

It's NOT an ADVENTURE until SOME-THING goes WRONG.

#LOVEORWORK

CHAPTER 1

# The Great Adventure

## ANDRÉ

**While we never quite know where journeys will take us, we can be confident that we will not return home the same. Often it takes encountering the journey of another to help continue our own. The best journeys, after all, are those that are shared.**

—ANDREW M. DAVIS

My dream since I was sixteen was to own a VW bus (aka a "Westy") and drive across the country. I pictured myself overlooking the Grand Canyon watching the sunset or parking on a beach and falling asleep to the sound of waves crashing onto the rocks.

It was my husband's dream to relax in a lounge chair at a pool next to the beach while servers brought him drinks. He would fall asleep listening to a podcast to block out the screams of our kids cannonballing into the water next to us.

One thing I learned very quickly about marriage: people vacation completely differently. Jeff looks at vacations as times of doing nothing, and I look for crazy adventures. We have learned the importance of allowing each partner to plan vacations so each of us can be filled in the specific way we need.

"You get to choose our next vacation," he said. And so I chose "the dream." We had been married for thirteen years, and our two kids were out of the baby stage. It felt like the right time for the dream to come true. I found a rental place in LA, and I even chose the color of the Westy in my dreams: old-fashioned blue. As we strolled into the LA garage, excited to see what was in store, we instantly realized that owning a Westy meant you would be constantly fixing a Westy (thank God this was only a ten-day rental).

The hippy owner welcomed us with great excitement. "You are in for the time of your lives," he exclaimed. "Your kids will talk about this experience forever!" Then we saw my dream car. It was beautiful. All of Instagram would be proud. It was a 1968 jewel in that pale blue color I envisioned, restored to perfection. From the retro curtains to the vinyl seats, the dream was finally real.

We chose an automatic transmission because it had been a while since I drove a stick (and that adventure in Nicaragua is another story for another day). The steering wheel was huge. The dashboard featured three components:

1. The vent (because maybe AC wasn't invented yet?)—either open or closed.
2. The radio with a CD player—obviously an upgrade that had been added. As a bonus, the glove compartment was fully stocked with '60s and '70s Americana albums.
3. The emergency lights button.

We were informed that day if we were going as fast as we possibly could go, we would be topping our speed at 55 miles per hour (and that was going *downhill*). We were also informed the gas gauge was a little fickle. "Just assume if it shows three-quarters tank it means full, and you can make it eightyish miles on a full tank," said the man who looked like he belonged at Woodstock. *Well, this will be interesting . . . but we've got this!*

We rolled down the windows with our hands and arm muscles (nothing was automatic on this baby), and we found places to store all our stuff. The owner even strapped a camping grill on top of the roof along with four camping chairs for our campsite destinations. We were ready.

Driving through downtown LA on the highway at about 40 mph was a little scary. People would be all road rage-y and whip over to pass us, then slow down next to us as they realized what we were driving. They would give us that head nod, as if to say, "Nice ride. You are living the dream." Yes, we were. We smiled and waved. Even when we would pull up to a four-way stop, every other car would give us the right-of-way, probably so they could take a moment to admire our Westy beauty.

We were feeling good and getting the hang of our new ride while my hair whipped all over my face from the open windows on the open road. Our kids were happily screaming and singing in the back seat. Best part? We couldn't hear them because of all the open windows. It was a parent's dream. We were heading out of LA to get to the Pacific Coast Highway, traveling north without a care in the world. About sixty-five miles in, we planned to stop at the next exit to fill up with gas. We were chugging up a hill—a big hill. Jeff's foot was pushed to the metal floor. We were huffing and puffing, traveling at a solid 35 mph, when all of a sudden the roaring motor stopped roaring. I instantly thought Jeff must be doing something wrong. But, no, everything appeared normal. Jada shouted from the back seat, "Why are we slowing down?" Neko yelled, "Are we going backwards?" Soon the old Westy began sputtering and, yeah, no longer moving forward. I knew this feeling (boy, do I know it well). We had run out of gas. I have run out of gas a hundred times in my lifetime (I know, I know, it's a problem). Jeff has not once run out of gas. He's one of those tank-full people—I've never understood it.

First day . . . first drive . . . out of gas.

We pulled the van over to the right side of the highway on a mountain that felt like a 55-degree angle pointed straight toward the skies. We rolled to a stop and turned on the emergency lights button (at least we had that button).

We decided to text the hippie owner. He would know what to do and how to help us.

He wrote back immediately.

"That sucks. Well, it's not an adventure until something goes wrong! Have fun."

*It's not an adventure until something goes wrong.* This quickly became our family motto. It was already sort of the story of my life.

Yes, I am one of those women whose plans have been consistently derailed (and haven't we *all* been derailed at some point?). I was a child of a missionary family. My life felt like it was filled with travel, adventures, and friends around the world: an ever-changing adventure I loved. One dreadful day my crazy life in South America came to a screeching halt, and my family moved back to the United States (for good this time). Life felt like it was over. After the glittering honeymoon period of enjoying McDonald's and normal-functioning toilets was over, I was bored. I vowed to myself, at the age of ten, that I would not become "American" and succumb to this life of wealth and privilege and "sameness."

As I was growing up as a teenager in the States, my parents instinctually realized I needed to leave the country—often. Luckily, they provided me opportunities to return to my Latin roots as often as possible. I spent summers and school breaks taking short trips to other countries. My grandparents lived in Puerto Rico, and I spent many spring and winter breaks with them.

Entering college, I was determined to live in the States

only to get my education, with the goal to leave as quickly as possible. Medicine seemed like an occupation I could practice anywhere, so pre-med was my ticket out. I was a woman on a mission to experience it all. Every opportunity for an adventure out of the ordinary brought a deep sense of joy to my soul. Every summer was spent in a different state or country. One summer was spent driving across the country with my best friends from Michigan to Washington with no job, no place to live, and only gas money to get there. We ended up house-sitting all summer (for a place to live) and finding random jobs (selling Cutco knives, cleaning mansions on Capitol Hill, taking care of farm animals, and bartending). A car given to us by a random church member ended up breaking down every other day (there was a lot of hitchhiking that summer), and we had the time of our lives. Another summer was spent in Kenya working at a clinic in one of the biggest and most dangerous slums in Nairobi and traveling with Samaritan's Purse to Southern Sudan during the war to help UNICEF care for immobilized child soldiers.

The adventures and travels brought deep joy, though my parents were often scared for my life and maybe didn't know all the dangers. I do believe they understood my free-spirited soul and wanted to let me fly. And fly I did. In my mind, nothing was going to hold me back: no man, no house with a white picket fence, and definitely no children. I wasn't going to settle down. I imagined myself as the next Mother Teresa (but Bolivian, with blond hair and blue eyes). I kept focused through college. I needed to keep my grades up, uphold my volleyball scholarship, and study endlessly through a vigorous pre-med program.

And then the unexpected happened. I met this relentless guy named Jeff.

We were never meant to be a match. He wanted to climb the ranks in corporate America. I wanted to grow gardens in Africa. He read books about leadership. I read books about hiking

Machu Picchu. He was a marketing guru at twenty years of age. I thought marketing only proliferated a culture built on consumerism. There was no way this would work. We were complete opposites. I fought his philosophy with my activism, his ambition with my conscience, and his pursuits with my mission—tooth and nail.

**André: For six months this poor man kept asking me out; every day I said no.**

Jeff: I always knew in the end you would say yes. I mean, we were meant to be together. Right?

**I wasn't even attracted to you. But you just kept showing up at my door wanting to hang out with me. It was actually kind of sad how many times I said no to you.**

I remember my roommate asking me if I was ever going to give up. Never. You and I would be up together until two in the morning drinking coffee at Dunkin' Donuts, and I would ask, "Hey, André, how about we continue this conversation over dinner tomorrow night?" And you continued to say no. Every. Single. Day.

**Some version of this conversation happened every day. For six months. The fight was real, people.**

Then one day you were all over me.

**[Eye roll] I probably wouldn't say it like that. More like you wore me down. I finally said yes. We fell in love.**

And you were all over me. I think our constant debates are what actually brought us together and in a weird way what always connected us, don't you?

**We fight a lot, that's for sure. Fire and ice. The likelihood**

**of us staying together is slim. That's how the Enneagram Institute explains our conflicting personalities.[1] (For those interested, I am a One and he is an Eight.)**

It also says if we can get on the same page, we could be part of changing a community, a city, or maybe even change the world! Now that sounds like an adventure.

*Sometimes love brings two unlikely and broken people together for one seemingly impossible adventure.* We call this marriage. Marriage did not fit into my original dream, and yet we married the summer after graduating from college. My adventure took a new direction.

Buying a house did not fit into my plan, and yet we bought a cute little house in Atlanta while I was in my master's program to become a physician's assistant.

Kids definitely were not supposed to happen, and yet we were adopting and loving a brown bundle of pure joy five years after landing my first job at an urban clinic in downtown Atlanta. And then two years after that, a little boy grew in my belly.

How did all this happen in ten years? How did all my plans derail from the script? Sometimes we have moments in life and wonder, "How did I get here, and do I even like what is happening? Am I truly happy?" I was thirty-two years old, ten years into marriage with two littles hanging on my arms, when I finally asked myself this question.

But I *was* happy.

I loved my job. I loved my kids. And most importantly, I still loved my husband. I was living a different adventure than what I imagined, and I wouldn't exchange it; I couldn't exchange it. Sometimes the greatest adventures begin through people we love; we can't make sense of it, yet we know we are better off because of it.

It was a life that made me happy, but all the responsibilities of work, family, and marriage were burdensome. Adulting is hard—can I get an amen? There were days—seasons—when I felt like I was losing myself.

We were going to a church at the time that seemed fairly modern and progressive, yet I observed nearly every woman stop working when they started having children. What was happening? Was it because we lived in the South? These were highly talented women with corporate experience at Coca-Cola, lawyers from Harvard, and teachers with expertise in transforming education, all with degrees that took them years to accomplish. I admired these women, and yet I couldn't see myself following in their footsteps. I was looking for a mentor, a hero, a modern woman to guide me because I felt overwhelmed and lost in the responsibilities of life. I had a passion for medicine, health, and wholeness. If I let this part of me go, I knew I would not be fully me. I was young and looking for a woman who could show me that *both* could be done. Family and work.

Arianna Huffington explained this well in an interview with Tim Ferriss, "Women should be given equal respect for whatever they choose to do in their lives. If they choose to have a career, everything should be open to them. If they choose to be a mother and they can afford to do that and choose not to have a career, they should be given equal respect for that."[2]

I believed that statement wholeheartedly, but it didn't take away from the cultural shame I was feeling from my environment. Truthfully, both camps today struggle with shame and insecurities. Career women struggle with the time away from their kids and families. They are always deliberating: Am I working too much? Do my kids need me more? Those who stay home with their kids often wonder if their lives are too wrapped up in their children. Do the children need more space and freedom? We women hold on to these areas of insecurity and join "camp stay-at-home mom" or "camp working mom," then judge women in the other camp instead of supporting each other. Everyone around me said I couldn't have it all, and as I looked at these amazing women, whom I respected, they showed me with their choices that maybe I couldn't. Love. Work. Family. They were telling me, "Choose one or two, but no way can you have all three."

My happiness began to turn more and more into a growing anxiety that I was not going to be able to hold it all together. Yet I needed to keep it together. Living in a big city was expensive. My work paid more money than Jeff's start-up nonprofit. My work provided health insurance. My work had a matching 401(k) plan. I was determined to keep my work, my family, and my Jeff.

I just needed to work harder. I was going to *will* all three to happen. I decided to prove them all wrong. If there is one thing I am, it is determined (also known as stubborn). I was not going to fail; failure wasn't an option. So my perfectionist spirit took over. I worked full-time, putting in fifty to sixty hours per week. I woke up at 5:30 to run with my training partner, then rushed home to get Jada ready for her Spanish immersion preschool, hoofed it to get to work on time, and dashed home to make a healthy dinner for Jeff and play with Jada before bedtime. Then I collapsed into bed with my computer to finish up on work before falling asleep to wake up and start the cycle all over again.

I was killing it (or so I thought). Until I wasn't. Until it all became too much. Until I could barely recognize myself anymore. Honestly, Jeff didn't recognize me anymore either. I was too tired for sex, too exhausted to have real conversations with him. I didn't even laugh anymore. I was merely existing. There was no adventure and no time for fun. I was definitely missing something. And Jeff and my family were missing me. But there was no time to listen to what I wanted or needed. I was lost in the doing. I was lost in being the perfect mom and keeping up.

The first few years of marriage, life was full of adventure and spontaneity, but those things were quickly being replaced with the sad reality of a Google calendar, work pressures, and a constant to-do list. One thing was true: I couldn't keep up with this pace in life. Something had to give.

It became clear that as an adventure-loving perfectionist, I was not going to be perfect at anything I loved. I was never going to be able to devote myself fully to all of the above and still enjoy life. I had to gain clarity on who I am and who I am not and come to grips with my limitations (more on this in chapter 7).

Here are some of my limitations I needed to accept (obvious now, but epiphanies at the time):

- It is impossible to work all day and then work at night as well.
- I cannot do this life without Jeff helping me and taking on a significant amount of the responsibilities for the kids.
- If I am going to care for my family, I must care for myself, not to check things off my to-do list, but to be quiet, listen, be outdoors, and rest.

I love my work, and most importantly, I love my patients. This is why I do what I do. I love hearing about their grand-babies and their constipation. I love having complicated sex talks with teenagers, who didn't realize they really could get an STD, and I love hugs and drooly kisses from the babies. Yet my patients cannot consume all my thoughts and time, or I won't have any mental and emotional space for the other people I love. Including me.

Not only do I love my work, but I love Jeff. Yet I refuse to be a woman who is wrapped up in her man, like what I do or don't do in life depends solely on Jeff. I love that man with all my heart, but I also love sushi nights with my girlfriends. I love my alone time with a book while swinging in my hammock. I love our date nights every week. I love doing life with the one person who knows me so well. He is truly my best friend. But I cannot lose me for him.

I also love my kids. There is a distinct honor in shaping the hearts and minds of my kids. I get to be a part of their maturity and growth. I have the privilege of guiding them into their own pursuits and passions. I don't want to miss any moments, yet I do, and I will continue to. Because no one can be there for every single thing that happens. I cannot kill myself to be their everything.

After having a lot of conversations with friends and mentors and reading Brené Brown's life-changing book *The Gifts of Imperfection*, I began to recognize a missing ingredient in my crazy life. It was called self-compassion. It began a journey of letting go of who I thought I was supposed to be and embracing who I am uniquely made to be. Brené Brown calls this "wholehearted living." She says, "Wholehearted living is about engaging our lives from a place of worthiness. It means cultivating the courage, compassion, and connection to wake up in the morning and think, 'No matter what gets done and how much is left undone, I am enough.' It's going to bed thinking, 'Yes, I am imperfect and vulnerable and sometimes afraid, but that doesn't change the truth that I am also brave and worthy of love and belonging.'"[3] Engaging my work, family, and marriage with this viewpoint was the catalyst that changed everything for me.

I remember having a conversation with my wise friend Phileena Heuertz during a time when I was exhausted and emotionally drained. She gently said, "André, you need to be kind to yourself." That thought had never crossed my mind at that point in my life. I knew how to be hard on myself, to push myself, and even to shame myself. But to be kind to myself? Mind. Blown.

Giving myself grace, asking myself what I truly needed, and showing myself compassion and self-love began the process of guiding me back to myself. I needed adventure, I needed to travel, I needed time to myself, I needed a quiet space, I needed prayer and meditation.

The question we all must ask ourselves in the journey of love, work, and family is not *if* we can maintain all three pursuits but *how* we can maintain these three overlapping purposes without losing our deepest self.

I realize many of my female friends also struggle with these tensions surrounding the desire to make an impact in this world beyond being a mom and wife. We have worked hard to get degrees in our specialized fields, we have fought against the patriarchy for positions in the business world, we have built organizations that are changing communities, and we are now the decision-makers in our companies. We are also having babies and families, and we don't want to leave the tables where we fought to gain a voice. I don't want to call us working moms—do we call men "working dads"? We are physicians. We are executives. We are educators. We are leaders. We are change-makers. And we have kids. And we are married. It isn't just me wrestling with the shame of working and struggling with the responsibility of being a mom and a partner. It is all of us. Here are some examples:

My friend who stays home with her kids confessed how much she missed her photography business. She missed the creativity. She missed meeting with clients and figuring out their style and vibe that she would capture on film.

Another friend, whose wife is a brilliant scientist and professor, decided to stay home with the kids while his wife pursued her career. He confessed his loneliness in this new role and difficulty as a man connecting with others during the day.

One friend told me she could not go to sleep at night without her phone next to her head; she was nervous that missing a call, email, or text could result in the end of her job. She and her new husband were only six months into marriage.

Another woman was running a small nonprofit organization and struggling to pay herself, which resulted in her and her partner not having a date night in over six months. (My sweet husband gave her money to take her hubby on a date that evening.)

Over the last few years, it seems we've consistently had these types of conversations every week. We began to realize this work-life tension issue is absolutely number one for many people, whether they recognize it or not. It's at least one of the greatest tensions in our community, and likely *the* greatest for many. We don't have all the answers and we're not the experts, but we do know the vital importance of voicing the tension and hearing all the perspectives in order to feel known and seen and to learn from each other.

My life looks nothing like what I imagined, and I often look back at my plan with longing—it was so simple! No husband, no kids, no attachments. Just me and my journey to love on others in need around the world. Sigh. How lovely and uncomplicated and straight-up dreamy. And here I am—all kinds of complicated. My journey started with one purpose and then the purpose expanded to include three others. I own a house, y'all! I have two children who depend on me to keep them alive. The grand plan for my life changed. It's not perfect, but it's imperfectly perfect for me.

I can still adventure, but now I do it with my three favorite people. I can still serve around the world, but now I have little ones watching with bright eyes and lots of questions. I might not be alone anymore, but I gained a best friend (who knows I also need my alone time). Life could not be any more different than what I imagined, and yet somehow it is exactly what it is supposed to be.

And that is exactly how I would describe our Westy adventure: imperfectly perfect. Let's go back to us chugging along the

PCH. We had found gas and were gradually making our way back to LA to return the Westy. It was the best vacation of my life. Not so much for Jeff. The way Jeff and I are opposites had become very evident along the way. Jeff looked for showers at each campsite, while I dipped in the ocean—"All clean!" Jeff wanted clean clothes, and I was fine with yesterday's. We're also an unlikely pair in how we plan. It was the last night of our adventure, and we had just finished ice cream with our friend Ali.[4] It was dark, and the kids were ready to go to sleep as soon as the sugar high had worn off.

André, did you seriously not reserve a campsite for our last night in this thing?

**First of all, don't call her a "thing"; she is our Westy, and you shouldn't hurt her feelings. And second, you know I don't like to plan every detail. Where's the fun in that?**

I don't understand where you expect us to just find a place to park and sleep tonight. It's already dark, the kids are exhausted, and I am so over this thing. Can I please just book us a hotel room?

**No way! We're going to find a beach, just like I dreamed.**

What? André, baby, you don't just find a beach and roll in. You have to reserve a site and plan for these things!

**Ye of little faith, I think I know a spot, and we'll pull right in undetected. It's late enough at night anyways. We won't even have to pay!**

You "know a spot"? You seriously drive me crazy.

And drive we did, to the perfect location for our last night in the Westy. Lo and behold, the final night of our great family adventure consisted of pulling up to the edge of the beach and slipping in between two forty-foot motor homes where we were lulled to sleep by the waves crashing onto the rocks. A natural white-noise sleep machine. Of course, it looked much different than I imagined in my dream, squished into a VW bus with one kid draped half across my body breathing his hot breath down my neck. But I wouldn't have exchanged it for anything.

The takeaway? Life is an adventure you have to work to find; no doubt that adventure will look a bit different—or more complicated—than what you first imagined.

## TALK ABOUT IT

Before you move forward, take a moment to answer these questions on your own and invite your partner to discuss them with you.

1. How has your original adventure of life taken a change in direction? Where do you think it is leading you next?
2. What differences do you have with your partner in choosing vacations? Who makes the choices, and how do you decide what to do and where to go?
3. Every time we recount our story of falling in love, it reminds us what brought us together. Think back to when you first fell in love. What brought you together? There are always two sides to the story.
4. What limitations do you struggle to accept on your journey of family life?

## DO A CHALLENGE

We all need creative ideas for taking what we read and putting it into practice. Share your experience with others and tag @loveorwork #loveorwork.

***Dream together.*** Have you ever made an adventure bucket list with your partner? Go out to dinner. Bring a clean piece of paper and a marker. Come prepared individually with ideas. While you eat, craft your bucket list together. What is something you want to do this year, in three years, in five years? Plan the date of your first adventure on the spot. Take it home and post your list somewhere significant in your house.

## LISTEN UP

Add to this journey by listening to a free podcast that relates to this chapter and will give you even more to process. Go to www.loveorwork.com/listenup.

**Visionaries, Entrepreneurs, and Dream Releasers: Jennie and Zac Allen (Episode 15)**

These two visionaries and entrepreneurs teach about how to keep pursuing your dreams even when it feels impossible and how to be a "dream releaser" for your partner. Jennie is an author and the founder of the IF:Gathering, and Zac is a serial entrepreneur.

IF WE CHANGE the WORLD and LOSE our FAMILY, we LOSE.

-ANDRÉ and JEFF SHINABARGER-

#LOVEORWORK

CHAPTER 2

# *Pick One*

## JEFF

**A good marriage is where both people feel like they're getting the better end of the deal.**

—ANNE LAMOTT

It's been another great year! I'm so excited to be here with you, let's celebrate tonight and talk about the past year and how our lives have changed.

**Yes, let's do that. It's been the worst year of my life.**

Wait. What?

It was our first weekend away as a couple since we became parents. Just the two of us. Eleven months earlier was the celebration of our adoption. It all happened extremely fast. One day we were filling out paperwork, and three months later we stared into the eyes of our tiny daughter in shock. I thought the adoption process would take three years. It took three months. There was no preparation and no adjustment time. We were thrown into parenting and diapers and sleepless nights without reading the "What to Do with a Baby" manual. It had been almost a full year of adjusting and learning how to be full-time working parents. Translation: one year of no one-on-one time with my wife. Which leads me back to the anticipation for this weekend away. *Finally!*

Our babysitter was prepped for the weekend, and as new parents we'd set up the house for any possible outcome she might encounter (i.e., famine, drought, hurricane, tornado, shark invasion). We boarded a plane to Austin, Texas, and had reservations at a swanky new restaurant to celebrate my thirty-first birthday. This night was going to be an amazing celebration of the past year and the positive changes in our life. I imagined that after our expertly curated farm-to-table dinner we would eat chocolate cake topped with a dramatic sparkling candle and the staff would serenade us into our grown-ups–only evening. We would go for a long walk exploring downtown and dream together about the next year. We had a great hotel room, including a full night's sleep at no extra charge, and no baby interruptions. It was going to be an adult weekend full of adults-only choices. Maybe we would get a massage. Maybe we would go to a movie. Maybe we would simply sleep in. This was going to be the best weekend ever.

Errr . . . maybe my expectations were a little off.

We sat down at our table, and before we even ordered drinks, it began. I instigated the conversation. My birthday dinner. Our romantic date night. I was ready with questions to deepen our rich dialogue about celebrating life together. André came to dinner with something totally different on her mind.

I had been looking forward to this time for months. She had been suppressing her feelings for months.

She continued with why it had been the worst year ever.

**I have made a ton of changes since we had a baby, and you have made no changes. Your work has taken priority over everything. You leave for three- and four-day trips. You come and go whenever you want. Do you think I am the only one who should be taking care of our baby? You're acting like this family is only my responsibility. This is not what I signed up for. I thought we were supposed to be partners. Instead, I am doing it all. I have dreams. I have work. I need a break. I am done with this. I am done.**

As you can imagine, as André's long-suppressed feelings came gushing out, the intensity and volume of the conversation grew too. There was a lot of yelling—and it wasn't coming from anyone else in the restaurant.

Uhhh . . . I don't know what you're talking about. You do remember this is my birthday, right? Can you just try to lower your voice a little bit? I thought adoption was your dream?

**Of course you would say that. It's all about your birthday. All you care about is yourself. All you care about is what others think. It's all about you. And adoption was *our* dream.**

Are you serious right now? I had to take on more work to pay for the adoption while you were on maternity leave. We couldn't have made it financially this past year without my work! You were able to stay home for three months, while I had to do twice the work to keep up with our bills.

**What? I never told you I wanted to be a stay-at-home mom. Is this how it's going to be? Do you think you**

**are the hero of this family? Hell no. You are doing the easy part . . . I am doing all the hard parts. Wiping butts. Getting up in the night. Every night. You have it easy. You are going out for work lunches, while I'm eating leftovers. You are going golfing, while I'm mixing together bottles. You are going on trips every week, leaving me feeling like I'm a single mom. Last time I checked, we were supposed to be partners.**

Sorry for choosing a profession with some side benefits. I have to do this stuff to grow the organization. Actually, no, I'm not sorry. This is what I am made to do.

**So what you are really saying is that your "purpose" is more important than mine—actually, it's more important than everything. So what's it going to be? Work or family? Your dream or your wife?**

We never ate. No cake. No sparkling candle. No singing. Crickets. We left the restaurant. Actually, she ran out of the restaurant, and I sprinted after her. It was the birthday dinner of no one's dream ever.

To be honest, I had no idea what she was talking about. I was embarrassed and shocked. I had no clue. And no chocolate cake.

We walked about five miles in a constant argumentative state. I think I saw every street in downtown Austin. Sometimes we talked. Sometimes yelled. Sometimes in silence. Sometimes in tears. There were steps that André walked solo. Moments when I was alone on a bench. Brighter moments when we broke through the hard, raw circumstance and attempted to hold hands.

Our adoption happened in a blink: we were matched on a Thursday and became parents the following Monday. My work schedule is usually planned six months in advance, and though we'd become parents in five days, I didn't deviate from my work schedule even though we experienced this gigantic change in our life.

Starting a family was a turning point in my life, her life, our life. I needed to realize and reflect on the fact that a future family was taking shape that wasn't based on traditional gender roles, individual aspirations, or simply "the way it has always been." As a man, I thought my role in our family was to be a provider, but in reality my wife was making more money than I was. As a dreamer, I allowed my ego to drive all my creative ambitions, but deep down I knew André's work as a physician's assistant, literally saving lives, was crucial to the community. At the heart of it all, I wanted the person I love most in the world to live out her potential for good in the world. The way we were living wasn't providing space for this to happen. We were at a crossroads.

The night of my birthday opened my eyes to the reality that we were entering into a different era of family structure. It wasn't the birthday present I hoped for, and I certainly didn't want it that evening, but it opened up a critical dialogue for André and me. That day solidified that we were going to move forward in a different way, a better way. Were we the only couple wrestling through this tension?

## THE EVERYDAY MOMENTS

The family of today doesn't look the way my family did when I was growing up. I am thankful to have grown up with two parents who are still married. My dad was a pastor, and my mom stayed home with the children. This situation worked for my parents, as it has worked historically for many families in the United States. But the family structure is changing into what I believe is a better, more equitable future for every family member. Personally, this shifting family structure and the way it is lived out in our family starts with me and the life choices I make to serve my family. There are a few moments in life when we choose what we will be about, how we will live, and what values we will esteem the most. My birthday was one of those concrete moments that caused a shift in my heart.

Every day I make constant choices between work, marriage, and kids. How do I choose between the three things I love most? How do I choose one over any of the others? Fast-forward ten birthdays from that wake-up call in Austin to a man who does it. Every. Single. Day.

The logistics look something like this:

Every day at 3:45 p.m. the three confront one another. I'm sitting in a meeting in my office. I glance at the clock and see that 345 combination and everything intersects. It's like the split screen in one of the episodes of the TV show *24*. Me. André. The kids.

School pickup is at 4:00. It takes fifteen minutes to get from my front door to the school's front door. I imagine my kids walking from their classrooms to the cafeteria where all the kids wait to be called to join their parents. I imagine being fifteen minutes late and my kids being the lonely children waiting to be picked up.

Screen change to André—white coat, stethoscope around her neck, in a small sterile room with a patient. She glances at her phone. I have not called yet. She knows that means I am not en route to get the kids.

I flash to my friend Angelo Spinola's[1] chilling words: "Think about what you want to be known for. Is it that you had a significant career or were a fantastic father? Why is it that we expect our families to be more flexible than our work?"[2]

If we're being honest, don't we really want both?

3:47: Thanks for nothing, Angelo (he's right, but the struggle is real). Run out of the meeting early.

3:50: Call back into the meeting on my cell from the car.

Put it on speakerphone. Drive— fast! "Sorry, everyone, what did I miss?"





3:55: Stop at the infuriating light that always takes forever.

4:02: Finish the meeting and say goodbye as I'm walking into school.

4:10: Get the kids in the car and call André. Wipe sweat from brow.

Hey, honey, I got the kids—kids, want to say hi to Mommy?

**How was school? Way to go, Jeff. Hey, could you pick up a couple things for me on the way home?**

Sure. Just text me what you need. I have all the time in the world.

4:15: Call back my team to give them one more thought on the meeting.

Everything usually works out. No one is left at school, dinner finds its way to the table, but who wins in this scenario? None of my favorite people. We managed to make it without an accident or children waiting alone. But there are no winners. How and who do we prioritize in an age when everything demands our time? The era of an eight-to-five job is over. The simplicity of separating a work phone and a home phone is rarely possible. The separation of life's most important roles is not as easy as it once was.

When is it work time, and when is it family time? We feel it and we struggle with it and we blur the lines. I blur them every day.

It seemed much easier before we had children. Now we have a kid look at us and say, "Will you put your phone down and play with me?" How long before we look at them and ask them to put their phone down to play with us? The line between work and love, work and family, is becoming the great dilemma of our generation. If we cannot separate work and family, are we ultimately failing both?

## HOW DID WE GET HERE?

In college we believed we could change the world. Maybe you can relate to our story. We were affirmed by this world-changing idea in our early twenties when a group of crazy guys created a film called *Invisible Children.* I believe they were the first of many to plot a new course of action for our generation. André and I were not satisfied with "normal" work. We wanted our work to contribute to a better world, and we wanted to help each other make that a reality.

We found more inspiration through people who seemed so close to us through the social sphere and TED-like inspirational talks. We started buying TOMS shoes and were inspired by the story of Blake Mycoskie. We resonated with the authentic story of Scott Harrison[3] when he created Charity: Water, and either we created a campaign for our birthday or a friend created one for theirs.[4] Bono challenged us through the ONE Campaign to care about poverty and introduced us to conscious consumption. We bought a Giving Key to put around our neck to show that we supported job training programs for the homeless.[5] What we wore, where we spent our money, and how we used our time were showing a new order of what mattered. André and I wanted to do something about the problems we saw in the world. We wanted to do it together. We were a couple committed to doing better in the world. And we were not the only ones.

The word *purpose* started emerging in every conversation, from Rick Warren's book, which millions read, to the name of an entire album by Justin Bieber. *Social justice* was not just a term; it became a required way of living. We believed that living without care for our neighbors, our planet, and the world was a one-dimensional life. We wanted more. We intentionally moved into a neighborhood where we were the minority. We formed relationships with people different from us. Soon our friends were from different cultures, different neighborhoods, different sexual orientations, and different ethnicities. These friends helped us see the world from a broader perspective. And all the while, we shared this perspective together: partners in love.

Most importantly, we started asking questions, started listening, started trying new things, started caring for people in the world. We started doing things about the social issues that we saw were wrong. We learned about empathy and action. We. Together.

In the midst of all this, the most amazing device found its way into our homes and lives: the smartphone. It connected everything important to us: friends, causes, websites, tasks, emails, calendars, songs, movies, money, statistics, workouts—and the list goes on. Just like all technology, it was meant to make life easier and better. Access to the entire world landed in our hands.

After finding love, we had babies. We gained responsibility for our children, and our responsibility to stay plugged in and doing good grew too. While we had no idea what we were in store for as we grew our family and how that would alter our lives, we also had no idea how work was defining itself in our home too.

This is where we find ourselves today. It's the crucial 3:45 p.m. moment. Are we going to make it? So we have begun asking questions. These are questions André and I have felt very personally in our own marriage and have asked throughout our community. Having children doesn't mean we can't still change the world, right? We still have all our passions; our children just need to come along for the journey—or can they?

One way we have committed to continuing this conversation

while developing community is through our organization called Plywood People. Plywood is a nonprofit in Atlanta that leads a community of start-ups doing good. Members of this community of social entrepreneurs and nonprofit leaders have given their lives to restoring broken systems and are doing it at great cost. They are rarely paid much money but feel such a deep responsibility toward restoration that they are willing to let "people over profit" drive their lives. They work long hours, feel responsible for others, and care about making things better for vulnerable populations around the world. When people make decisions like this, the world around them takes notice. We are all wowed by their selfless pursuits to help others. You probably know people like this. They are leading emerging social enterprises ("businesses with a cause"), starting homes for women in prostitution, caring for the homeless, adding children to their families through foster care, and maybe even welcoming new refugees into the country. Their creativity toward solving problems is endless, and the fears they have overcome to bring these ideas into reality are many.

Meanwhile, alongside their heroic pursuits, often their personal lives falter. How do you change the world and still be a great father or mother?

Even more challenging, our culture now does this unique thing called "platforming." When you are a person overcoming fear for the good of others, our culture gives you a microphone. You start speaking and sharing your story. You start getting invited into the important rooms to tell the good news of your work. Your work is affirmed through applause, invitation, and celebration. Often the applause for our work is greater than the applause at home. As the applause gets louder, the invitations increase. You attend more influential meetings. All this is good, all this is important, all this is world-impacting. Good stuff that requires you to be away from home, to miss the 3:45 pickup. Good stuff that throws love of family off balance.

In the blink of an eye, sustaining a healthy work life takes over sustaining a healthy home life. And the lines are blurred. Work meets love. Work takes time from family. Family takes time from work. If there's no balance, what do we do? Is there such a thing as work-life balance?

What do you do when everything becomes work? Everyone becomes work. And the work becomes work. People want to go to meals with us and discuss work. Friends ask you about your work. Family helps support your work. Work becomes life and life is made possible through work. Where's the love? Where did the family go?

As meaningful work is becoming a more desired way to live and as the freelance culture is becoming a normal way to make ends meet, there is a confusing overlap and integration of mission, work, family, side hustle, friends, coworkers, marriage (and the list keeps going) that we all are wrestling with daily. Does work ever end if it is connected to your purpose? Not really. It just goes with us and moves to another conversation. It keeps expanding into all facets of our lives. We can't just hope things will be different; we have to be intentional about creating new ways to operate given this dilemma.

In the midst of all this work, there is a stark reality, often a tension, that you didn't put the work in at home. I didn't get the birthday present I expected eight years ago, but I got a glimpse into what happens when there's a work/family mismatch: we have to do good work and do good things for our family. We must create new patterns of operating.

## WHICH ONE WINS WHEN?

When faced with two good things, how do you decide which one wins? Sometimes when we care deeply about problems around us, we end up creating problems for those closest to us. We don't mean to, but it happens. Sometimes our dream, purpose, and meaningful work negatively impact our marriage and our kids. Why do we use up all our time and energy on our work and expect our family to accommodate our pursuits?

This was the crux of the epic "birthday fight" in Austin. I expected André to accommodate and cater to my dreams and work, without asking her permission. That moment is when I finally realized my selfishness in thinking my work was the most important. From that time I have constantly wondered if there is a better way or a different way.

Mother Teresa once declared, "If you want to change the world, go home and love your family." It's a great perspective from a person who often experienced the effects of the home in her clinics. Most believe that her family was the Church and her mission, the poor and vulnerable. Yet maybe she was on to something. She chose not to have a family for a reason. If I wasn't married, if I didn't have children, could I do more good in the world? Let's play out a couple of the other relational frameworks to consider.

*Can you do more good in the world as a person not in a committed relationship?* People asked Saint Francis if he ever thought about being married, and he spoke of "a fairer bride than any of you have ever seen," referring to his "Lady Poverty." John Wesley believed that more good could be accomplished if he focused on his relationship with God and the calling of his work, which led him to stay single for forty-eight years. And of course one of the noblest servant leaders of the twentieth century, Mother Teresa, chose to care for people who were dying in Calcutta over a life of marital relationship. Though she believed in the traditional family unit fiercely, she sacrificed having a spouse and children for the greater good of her mission. Years after her death, a book called *Come Be My Light*, a collection of her writings, depicted her deepest torment, referred to as the "dark night of the soul." Even she struggled for over fifty years in a spiritual wilderness and deep loneliness. Had her work taken over?





Most people at a very core level are lonely,[6] which prompts the desire for a partner in life. I resonate with this. I would not be the person I am today without my life partner. We are better together. André sees things in me—good and bad—that I could never see in myself. Or maybe I can see them but am not willing to accept them. I know I can contribute more good to the world because I have found this partner who makes me better. Relationships can both *distract* us from our purpose and help us *discover* our purpose.

For some people, being single is a great gift for social change and includes luxuries few actually think or talk about. But most people reading this book have probably chosen the route of having a committed partner (or wanting one in the future), and so we will make an assumption that most reading are looking for love through relationships.

*Can you do more good in the world as a couple with no children than as a couple with children?* There are three couples we know personally who have proactively chosen not to have children for this specific reason. Our podcast with Chris and Phileena Heuertz[7] taught us so much about this decision as a sacrificial concept.[8] Their conviction is that their life mission would be held back if children were their daily responsibility. While things can always change, they could not travel, serve, or lead in the same way with kids.

Now, others have tried hard to have children and experienced loss, failed pregnancies, and failed adoptions. If that is your story, we want to extend empathy and great respect to you. Though you may grieve not having the family you imagined, your circumstances may present a new way to engage the world as a couple.

## THE DREAM OF HAVING IT ALL

We want to love our partner and work with purpose and raise our family—we want to do it all. But if we're honest, most of us struggle to do all these things well. If we look into the greatest social change agents in history, we find that many of them gave their lives to important work at the cost of their families and relationships. Yet we celebrate them as heroes. In many scenarios, the known social leader has been given priority to pursue their purpose and a partner has been given the responsibility of raising the family. Nelson Mandela fought for his mission, and his family missed having a father while he served in prison for twenty-seven years. Dr. Martin Luther King Jr. was the leader of the civil rights movement, and his family lost a husband and father for the sake of the cause. I could go on giving examples of families that suffered for a greater purpose.

Some may say the greatest way for kids to understand purpose is for their parents to show it with their own lives. Yes.

Some may say the greatest thing parents can do for their kids is to have a healthy marriage. Yes.

Some may say the greatest way to change the world is through raising kids who change the world. Yes.

We believe that if we change the world and lose our family, we lose.

We are on a mission to unpack the hope that we can simultaneously pursue our purpose, stay in love, and raise world-changing kids.

We are on a journey to answer this unique question for ourselves, for those currently grappling with this tension, and for a new generation. We want to learn from others and share our findings with those of you who also feel the strain between love and work. In the next chapter André will share what our research has revealed about the challenge of managing our personal and professional lives.

## TALK ABOUT IT

Before you move forward, take a moment to answer these questions on your own and invite your partner to discuss them with you.

1. Like Jeff's 3:45 p.m. example, share a time when you felt like all three aspects of work, marriage, and children collided at one specific moment and how it made you feel.
2. In your marriage, how has the structure of your family of origin impacted your view on work and life balance?
3. How would you respond to Angelo Spinola's questions: "Think about what you want to be known for. Is it that you had a significant career or were a fantastic father [or mother]? Why is it that we expect our families to be more flexible than our work?"
4. How, if at all, do you feel the tension of work, marriage, and family in your own life? If there is a tension, what strategies help ease it and what compounds it?

## DO A CHALLENGE

We all need creative ideas for taking what we read and putting it into practice. Share your experience with others and tag @loveorwork #loveorwork.

***Explore your family of origin.*** Take a moment to draw out your family tree. Add to the side any mentors and influential people in your life. Next to each person write one to three characteristics regarding the way they balanced love and work. Take a moment to consider how the example they lived has impacted the way you operate today. What are three characteristics you want your family to attribute to you?

## LISTEN UP

Add to this journey by listening to a free podcast that relates to this chapter and will give you even more to process. Go to www.loveorwork.com/listenup.

**How to Disagree and Not Leave: Yvette and Glen Henry (Episode 98)**

Listen to this podcast to hear from a couple who, after months of coming home unhappy, decided to change their story. Glen decided to be a stay-at-home dad, which turned into his most purposeful work and led to the creation of Beleaf in Fatherhood.

The conversation is changing in **marriage** from if we can have it all to how we will maintain it all.

—André Shinabarger—
#LoveorWork

CHAPTER 3

# *Yes, But*

## ANDRÉ

**Love itself is what is left over when being in love has burned away, and this is both an art and a fortunate accident.**

—LOUIS DE BERNIÈRES

It all started in an Airstream. You've seen it—the iconic, silver bullet-looking Americana trailer.

One day our friend Brittany Thoms, who helps lead social media strategy for Airstream, called us.

**Brittany:** Remember that project y'all have been thinking about for a while now?

**Me:** Which one? (Jeff has a hundred projects happening at any moment.)

**Brittany:** You know, the one about the tension between work, marriage, and family? Remember, you told me you were thinking of interviewing people?

**Me:** Uh, I guess. You know that was just an idea, right?

**Brittany:** Yeah, well, I pitched that idea to Airstream as part of our Endless Caravan project. And, well . . . they are in!

**Me (pausing):** In for what?

**Brittany:** Loaning you an Airstream trailer so you can travel around the country to start interviewing people!

**Me:** Wait. What? When?

This conversation happened on a Tuesday, and the following Thursday we were on a plane headed to the Airstream headquarters in Jackson Center, Ohio. After an impressive tour where we learned all about this American-made company, they walked us to the parking lot to meet our new home away from home. The enormous monster awaiting us in all its glory took my breath away: there sat a huge big-wheel Ford F-150 attached to the twenty-four-foot-long silver beauty. In total it was a forty-foot rig. Can I just insert here that we drive a Toyota Prius (which is fourteen feet in length)?

We test drove it for one mile down a long straight country road. They instructed us how to unhook from and attach to the truck (one time). They shook our hands and said good luck.

Warnings and red flags flew through my brain: *We live in a big city! How do you drive this thing with traffic? What about parking? Oh my gosh, will this thing even fit in our driveway?*

But they were done with training and waved us off like proud parents. I stared at Jeff with what looked like the big-eye emoji face.

"Well, babe," Jeff said, "you love adventure! I guess this is our next one. Let's do this."

The next day we drove it back to Atlanta. We were thirty miles down the road when it dawned on us that we were driving a trailer and a truck worth about $150,000!

Did they really trust us? Because I didn't trust us. As we maneuvered "Big Dog" (our loving nickname for the silver beast) on the highway back south, we created an Instagram account, @loveorwork. We posted a video and asked people who we should meet. Who should we learn from? And where should we go?

The response was immediate. The recommendations came in from all over the country. The adventure began. We became weekend warriors. We drove Big Dog through the carpool lane every Friday to pick up our kids from school, and off we went every weekend for two months interviewing people for this new project called Love or Work. Let the fun begin!

## NOT JUST STORIES BUT FACTS

Weekend by weekend we interviewed couples. Another story, another interview, another point of view. The stories were adding up and we saw common threads in the responses to our questions. Similar concepts of how to build a healthy life where love *and* work were possible were bubbling up. There was a story here that needed to be shared.

We conducted one hundred interviews. While a small sample size, it's a massive amount of transcribing alone—not even getting into the thick of data analysis. We were committed in every situation to making sure *both* sides of the story were represented in the interviews to allow, what Paul Harvey made famous, "the rest of the story."

As we rambled along from interview to interview, in the back of my scientific brain, I kept thinking, "This is not enough information to make an accurate assessment." I'm a closet nerd, what can I say? But humor me (and my geeky self): one hundred subjective stories is helpful, but what if we surveyed a much larger group of people to understand more deeply this navigation of love and work? Enter: stats.

We partnered with Barna Group, a leading research organization focused on the intersection of faith and culture. We instantly connected with Brooke Hempell, senior vice president of research at Barna and a working mom with two young children. "I want to do this," she said. "This is exactly the tension I feel on a daily basis, and I am so interested in the data we could uncover."

Maybe you are reading this thinking, "That is *not* me; I don't like reading research and analytics. I'm going to skip ahead to the next chapter." Hold on! Wait one minute. I promise you (1) the report here will be short and to the point, and (2) the description of the data will be super easy breezy. Fascinating and surprising findings emerged, and we don't want you to miss them. These findings will impact how you navigate your own love and work.

For you data junkies who might want to know more about our findings, the full report is available online for your inquisitive minds at www.loveorwork.com/research.

## THE WHO

And now about the who. No, not the rock band, the demographics. First, let's clarify *who* we surveyed: 1,501 committed couples, 1,227 married, and 274 in long-term committed relationships. All were between the ages of twenty-five and fifty, lived in urban and suburban areas, and had an annual household income greater than $40,000. Two-thirds had children at home. In general, the group we surveyed were middle-class, dual-income families. Yet even with this specific demographic, there are wide implications for *all* who are navigating this world of love versus work.

PROFILE OF WORKING COUPLES

81% MARRIED
19% LONG-TERM RELATIONSHIP
21% HAVE BEEN DIVORCED

AGE BETWEEN 25-50
67% KIDS <18
33% NO KIDS <18

34% EARN < $75K
27% $75-100K
39 % $100K PLUS

## THE SHOCKING TRUTH

I am quite the cynic, so reading how positively people viewed the influence of their work on their kids and marriage surprised me (and made me gag just a little). But it also made me want to grab that fluffy blanket of positivity and curl up in the thought that all is right in the world (who knew research could do that?).

83% OF COUPLES SAY THAT WORKING HAS MADE THEM BETTER PARENTS.

*Record screech.* Wait. What?

That was the last thing I expected to uncover with this survey. I imagined that working made everything more difficult in the home. That working plus kids' schedules, practices, activities, homework, and general chaos made parents crazier, not better. This statistic might be encouraging to any of you without kids. Jeff and I waited eight years to have children because I was terrified I wouldn't be able to continue the work I loved. I guess this is my proof that you can work *and* be a great parent. And for those of you who feel guilty about working while raising kids, maybe this finding can allow you to take a deep breath. Maybe even stop and question if this is true for you.

When I think of my own life, I see that work has given me a purpose, a place (away from home) where I can use my gifts to contribute to a community beyond my bubble. Work tethers me back to myself, the person I was before kids, the person I am and always will be, the person who seeks justice for the oppressed, who uses medical knowledge to heal, who fights for those who are overlooked in society. When I return home at five o'clock and find myself in the mundane of cleaning house, cooking dinner, and folding laundry, I am reminded that this is not all of me. This is not my whole life. This is a part of me, but not all of me. Work is a part of me, but not all of me either. They both have their significance in my life in different ways, and they both matter.

Besides a majority of couples believing that working has made them better parents, here's another positive and significant finding. Remember that big question we're asking every couple we interview? *Is it possible to change the world, stay in love, and raise a healthy family?*

95% OF COUPLES BELIEVE IT *IS* POSSIBLE TO SIMULTANEOUSLY HAVE A CAREER, STAY IN LOVE, AND RAISE A HEALTHY FAMILY.

That is the highest affirmative answer out of all fifty questions we asked in the survey. People were so positive about this that I was blown away. And when we've asked every couple we've interviewed, their responses have matched the stat. But the responses have always included a *but*.

## YES, BUT . . .

The *but* has to be included, right? Everyone is positive about the work-love-family triad, yet they feel the contrasting tension. If you listen to our podcast, you have heard almost every single couple answer with:

Yes, but it's hard.
Yes, but something has to give.
Yes, but you have to stay healthy.
Yes, but you need help.
Yes, but you need marriage counseling.
Yes, but you have to plan and communicate.
Yes, but you need time to rest.
Yes, but you need to feel supported by your partner.

Here are some of the tension points the survey uncovered that confirm the qualitative data from our interviews.

**Yes, but it's hard.**

52% OF WOMEN (41% OF MEN) WHO WORK AND HAVE CHILDREN SAY THEY ARE EXHAUSTED.

---

45% OF WOMEN (28% OF MEN) WHO WORK AND HAVE CHILDREN SAY THEY ARE OVERWHELMED.

NEGATIVE FEELINGS ABOUT WORKING AND PARENTING

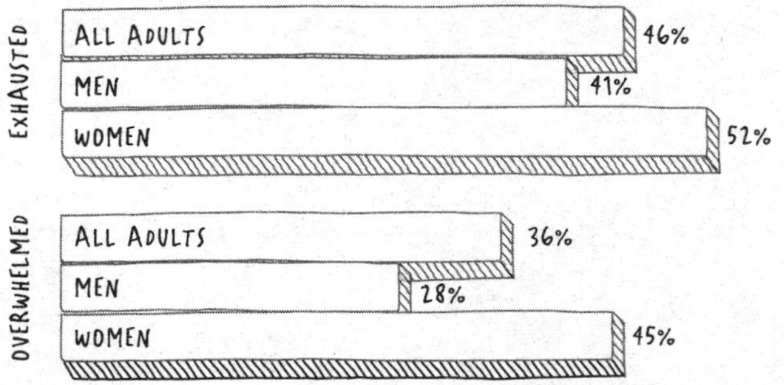

EXHAUSTED
ALL ADULTS 46%
MEN 41%
WOMEN 52%

OVERWHELMED
ALL ADULTS 36%
MEN 28%
WOMEN 45%

So we *think* we can do it, but we are exhausted trying. About half of women are exhausted and overwhelmed. Notice, this is true about the *women with children*. Aahhh, the days without kids when we had endless energy. And when we were tired, well, we could Netflix and chill all day if we wanted. No dependent little humans would stop us! Those of you with kids all know this fatigue. Your sleep depends on whether the kids sleep, your happy spirit depends on whether the kids had a good day, and your tired level after work doesn't matter because you have to dig into your energy stores to finish the day well with them. Kids are never-ending energy suckers. But we *all* can feel dead tired, even those of us without kids, because *time is a limited resource for everyone*.

And not only do we feel the fatigue, but we also understand the sacrifices.

**Yes, but something has to give.**

25% OF MEN SAY THEIR SPOUSE HAS SACRIFICED THEIR WORK/INTERESTS FOR THEIR JOB AS COMPARED WITH 13% OF WOMEN WHO SAY THEIR SPOUSE HAS SACRIFICED FOR THEM.

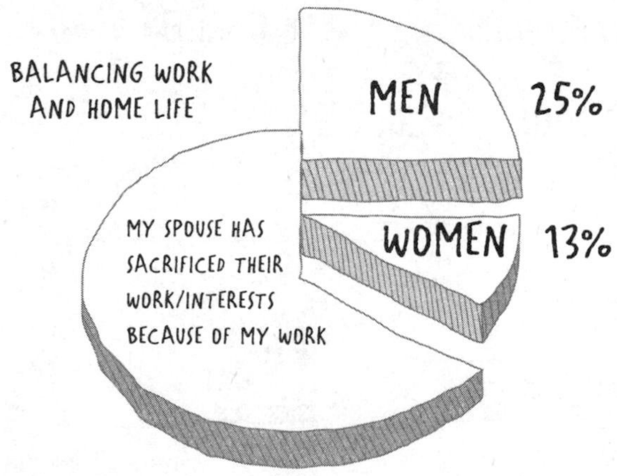

Interesting.

That statistic right there says a lot, doesn't it? It stirred up a lot of questions within me. Why are women sacrificing their work more than men, almost twice as much? Are we still following gender norms in regard to work? Whether we're looking at the 25 percent or 13 percent stat, aren't those *low* percentages? Something has to give, but who is actually giving and sacrificing?

If you are feeling all fired up about this statistic, don't worry—we'll unpack these questions more in future chapters.

**Yes, but you have to stay healthy.**

29% OF PEOPLE ARE VERY SATISFIED WITH THEIR PHYSICAL HEALTH.

---

39% OF PEOPLE ARE VERY SATISFIED WITH THEIR SPIRITUAL WELL-BEING.

---

41% OF PEOPLE ARE VERY SATISFIED WITH THEIR MENTAL/EMOTIONAL HEALTH.

---

21% OF PEOPLE ARE VERY SATISFIED WITH THEIR FINANCIAL SECURITY.

Let's review these statistics: Only about one-third of the people we interviewed are very satisfied with their physical and spiritual health, and less than half with their mental and emotional health. And though *both* partners work, only 21 percent are very satisfied with their finances. Yikes.

These areas of health and self-care are what get lost in the

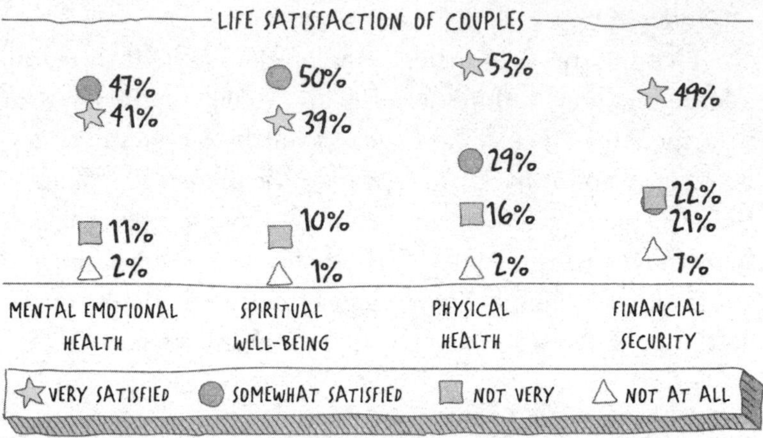


shuffle of trying to make it all work. As dual-income parents trying to contribute to our purpose, we do everything we can to maintain all our responsibilities yet lose ourselves for the sake of the cause. This is where we are losing; this is where we are sacrificing. This is why we are exhausted.

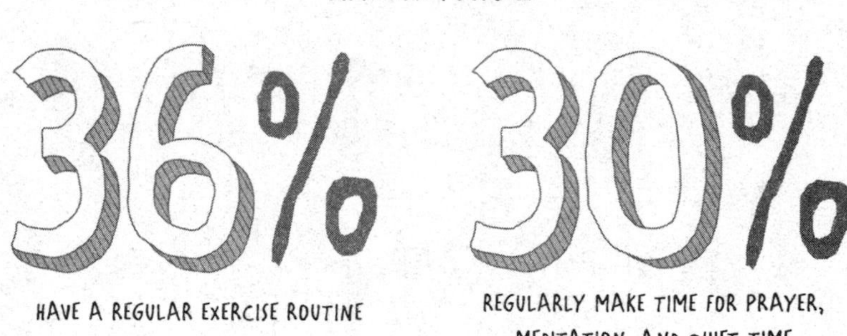


Most likely you struggle with staying healthy physically, spiritually, and emotionally too. We try so hard to make it all work. We work hard. We love our spouse. We love our kids. We do it all. We sacrifice. We just sacrifice ourselves.

39% OF WORKING COUPLES DO NOT RELY ON ANY OUTSIDE HELP.

---

9% OF WORKING COUPLES USE A HOUSE-CLEANING SERVICE.

---

15% OF WORKING COUPLES USE A GARDENING/YARD WORK SERVICE.

---

15% OF WORKING COUPLES USE DAYCARE/AFTER-SCHOOL PROGRAMS.

---

5% OF WORKING COUPLES USE A PART-TIME NANNY.

---

4% OF WORKING COUPLES USE A FULL-TIME NANNY.

We need help, and about 60 percent of the couples interviewed did use some kind of outside help. Which is reassuring. However, 39 percent said they don't have any outside help. If you are in this category, you need all the prayers. I don't know how you are doing it, but I'm sure you are struggling.

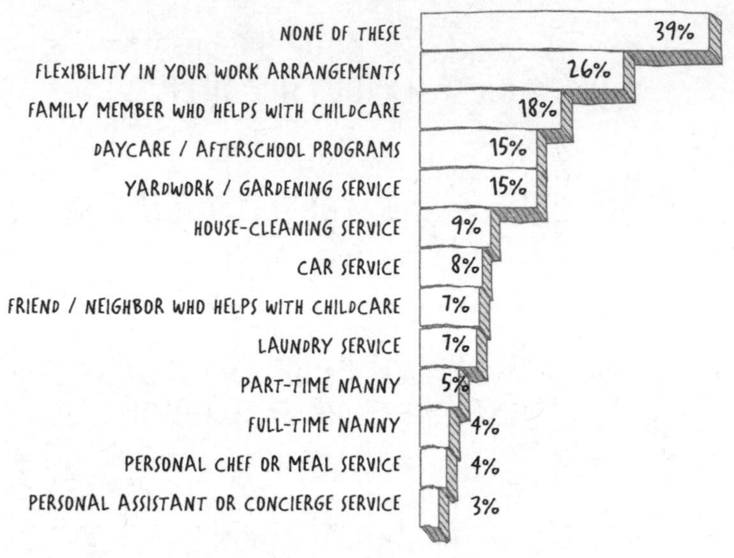


**Yes, but you need marriage counseling.**

## 8% OF WORKING COUPLES HAVE GONE TO A COUNSELOR FOR MAINTENANCE.

*Every* healthy couple we interviewed told us how maintenance counseling was essential to their health and longevity as a couple. Yet so few of the general population avail themselves of counseling! I know there are barriers. I have felt them all myself. The cost. The time. The question of which counselor is right for me. The struggle is real, so I can understand this low percentage. But *wow*, that is a low percentage.

**Yes, but you have to plan and communicate.**

As a planner, I think these statistics are insanely low. How in the world can two individuals who both work and have their

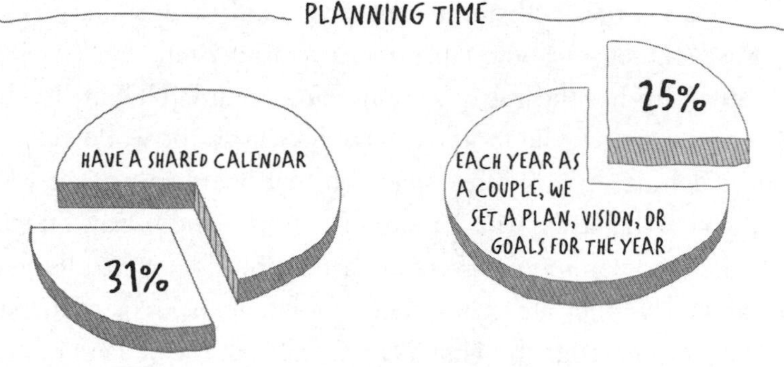


own social calendars, as well as their kids' social/school/activities calendars, *not* share a calendar? My anxiety level is rising just thinking about it. About 70 percent of couples do not share a calendar. Astounding.

**Yes, but you need time to rest.**

41% OF PEOPLE USE ALL THEIR VACATION.

This stat means that about 60 percent of those surveyed do *not* use all their vacation. I am not sure I understand why. Aren't vacation days like the free spaces on a bingo board? They are freely given, and we get paid for those days! So why in the world are we not snatching up every free space on that board so we can yell "Bingo!" at the beach with a margarita in our hand? Okay, I'll tell you the most common reason our participants do not use all their vacation days: they are saving them (for emergencies or sickness). Listen, if you or your child has a chronic illness, I get it. I am in the medical field, and illness is a difficult roadblock. However, if this is not your family scenario, consider whether saving vacation days is a fear-based decision. The "just in case" scenarios often don't happen. Therefore, you are missing beautiful moments with your family *right now* for something that may never occur.

**Yes, but you need to feel supported by your partner.**

ONLY 3 IN 10 PEOPLE FEEL ENCOURAGED BY THEIR PARTNER TO PURSUE THEIR WORK AND DREAMS.

This statistic hurts my heart. As couples on the same team, only about 30 percent of people feel encouraged by their partner to go after their dreams! This number needs to be higher, and we hope that as you continue reading this book, you will learn how such encouragement is vital to the health of your relationship.

Now that you see the big picture and the basics of the research, we want to go deeper and get into nitty-gritty real-life stuff with you in these next chapters. Since most of us are idealistic and believe we *can* simultaneously work, stay in love, and raise healthy families, the question now is not *if* we can do it but *how* we can do it.

## TALK ABOUT IT

Before you move forward, take a moment to answer these questions on your own and invite your partner to discuss them with you.

1. Which findings from our research jumped out at you most? Why?
2. What strategies do you find make you a stronger parent?
3. Are you sacrificing your personal health in some way? How could you find ways to support each other for a healthier lifestyle?
4. Do you share a calendar, or can you think of other organizational strategies that would be helpful in navigating between work and family?

## DO A CHALLENGE

We all need creative ideas for taking what we read and putting it into practice. Share your experience with others and tag @loveorwork #loveorwork.

***Make the research personal.*** Sometimes when we read data, we think, "That's not true for me or my friends." Prove it. Pick one statistic from our research that surprised you. Ask friends the question and see what you learn. Do your friends use a shared calendar? Do your friends use their vacation days? How many of your friends feel exhausted, and what do they do about it? You may be surprised not only by the results but by the vulnerable conversations that transpire.

## LISTEN UP

Add to this journey by listening to a free podcast that relates to this chapter and will give you even more to process. Go to www.loveorwork.com/listenup.

**Importance of Intentionality: Brooke and Christian Hempell (Episode 73)**

In this episode you will hear more from Brooke, who led the research for this project. She and her husband both work and share how they intentionally make decisions together. They discuss when to say yes and no and how to handle work travel.

Learning to love the purpose of your partner is one of the greatest gifts you can ever give.

—Jeff Shinabarger
#LoveOrWork

CHAPTER 4

# *Three Love Stories*

## JEFF

**Work is a constant conversation. It is the back-and-forth between what I think is me and what I think is not me. . . . Like the person to whom I am committed in a relationship, it is constantly changing and surprising me.**

—DAVID WHYTE

"I love you," I blurted out suddenly.

I stared at her, waiting. And then waited more. Seconds passed, then minutes, and . . . nothing.

The three words had just slipped out. Granted, I was young and impulsive. And I had never experienced such powerful feelings before.

But my vulnerable words were followed with *silence*. André stared at me with her mouth closed. I wanted to pull my words back in like they were attached to my tongue.

No response. *Ouch.*

There were exactly three restaurant options for young people after midnight in Jackson, Michigan. Our late-night options were to grab a Grand Slam at Denny's, a burger and string fries at Steak 'n Shake, or coffee at Dunkin' Donuts.

Tonight we chose to sit in the parking lot of Dunkin' Donuts with the heat on blast while the snow flurried outside our windows. We were in post-coffee chill mode (also known as making out). My car was conveniently parked in the back of the lot; I was in the driver's seat with André next to me. We gazed into each other's eyes. I said what I honestly felt, what I wanted to say but probably wasn't quite ready to say. It just happened.

"I didn't mean to say that," I fumbled, trying (and failing) to correct the awkwardness. I had never said those three words to another human before. I may have said it to my parents, but not really; it was always more of a "love ya."

She gave me a smirk. And then, "Thank you."

*Wow.* Easily the most vulnerable moment of my life, and all I got was kind appreciation in return. And I hate this bit of confession: *it made me want her even more.* I picked up my cup of coffee, took a sip, put the car in drive, and headed home. *What did I just do? Will she ever say it back? Did I voice my feelings too quickly? Did I create separation with those three words?*

André was my first love. We were twenty years old. It would be two more years until we were married, but that night I doubted things would continue. Later I would learn she secretly knew she was in love with me too. The tough collegiate volleyball player I fell in love with was just scared. One glorious day, she would eventually tell me she loved me. And all would be right with the world again.

## OUR LOVE STORIES UNITE US

Whenever we sit with a new couple, we always start with what unites us: "How did you fall in love?" Everyone has a love story. There is something truly special about the fall-in-love moment.

Inviting couples to share theirs allows us to peel back the layers and remind them of the reason they care so much about the hard work of love.

*Was it the other's constant laughter?*

*Was it the challenging banter?*

*Was it the joy in joint activities?*

*Was it the other's quiet persistence?*

Over hundreds of conversations with couples, we've found that question often leads to a predictable series of responses.

First, a wonderfully honest shared smile from both partners. They often look at each other with that gaze of wonder and purity. And then there is a second smirk they sometimes give each other—because there are always two sides to the story. Their gazes silently communicate who will share their side first, while the other waits patiently for their agreement or rebuttal.

Just the simple act of asking couples to share their love story *instantly* brings them together; often they even physically snuggle closer. And when they start sharing, we are invited into their story. The stories are rarely utopian-perfect. Most couples have two very different perspectives on the same history. The A side and the B side—those didn't fade out with cassette tapes—and the story only gets better (and maybe a bit more exaggerated) with time.

Every couple has a unique love story, and every love story is *dualistically perfect.*

## OUR SECOND GREAT LOVE

André is my first great love. But like most people, I have another great love.

It's hard to determine who gets my greatest attention at any given moment in a day. There's a good chance this "other love" demands you to share your time and attention too. Research says the average American spends the majority of their life with this second great love: work.

Our generation has more expectations to be productive and available and responsive and, let's face it, wed to work than any previous generation. We have conference calls, text messages, email alerts, Slack channels, social streams, direct messages, and whatever new technology emerges between now and the time you finish this sentence. Our working culture expects us to be "on" and available days, nights, and weekends (and even vacations). Access is all the time and everywhere. When we go home, our minds are often still at work. When we go on vacation, 66 percent of Americans continue to work. We work and communicate constantly.[1]

Technology and accessibility offer some positives: André and I can text each other from work. We can check in with each other via a quick call at least once per day. I get emails from my kids' school that need immediate attention in the middle of a meeting. Communication between all our loves is integrated in everything we do. Yet technological advancement provides a way for work to infiltrate home life with more ease as well. Often there's no "clocking out" when you walk out the door. And this tension grows ever more complicated.

I love what I do, and I don't feel bad saying this.

André is the first love in my life. I love who I am meant to be with, and I love what I am meant to do. Some days these two loves have a rhythmic flow and work seamlessly together. Other times, however, balancing these two loves is an utterly frustrating battle, depending on the day's demands. Sometimes the emotional demands of my work can create distance from my family. Often, because you find purpose in your work, setting boundaries around your work can be difficult. When you do purposeful work, emotional connection to it happens naturally.

## PURPOSE VERSUS WORK

Let's first clarify work and purpose. Work and purpose can be two very different things. For some people purpose is woven throughout work, while for others work is just about getting a paycheck. More and more people today want purpose integrated with their work. If we're going to put in ninety thousand–plus hours of work in our life spans (forty-five years of forty-hour work weeks), we want our work to mean something. Our research shows 94 percent of our respondents feel a sense of purpose in the work they do, while 60 percent are "made for" or "called to" the work they do.

I think if the conversation were as simple as choosing between the love of your life and a boring job, everyone would be lined up for love. But when more and more people are doing work with meaning, the work is hard to turn off and its presence bleeds into love. I want to live for a reason. I want purpose.

What is my reason for existence? This daunting question is one everyone asks at some point in their life. We want to discover whatever it is that defines our unique contribution to the world. French philosophers have called it "raison d'être," and some spiritually minded friends refer to it as a "calling." The Japanese named it *ikigai*.[2] Here's one way to figure it out: what is your sweet spot that brings together what you love, what you are good at, what the world needs, and what you can get paid to do? Purpose has to do with using the abilities you have to solve the problems you feel called to address. When you can combine these categories, you will find your purpose.

Our research indicates a majority of people seek (and find) purpose or a sense of calling in their work. Yet for me, finding my second love was a long, tenacious process, and I would not have found it without the encouragement, pushback, and insight of my first love. Finding purpose was something we had to work on together: we helped each other discover what we were individually and uniquely meant to do. Usually the person closest to us understands more about our giftings than we can comprehend ourselves. One of the greatest gifts a partner can bring you is helping you find clarity in the pursuit of your purpose.

In my work, I sit with many "idea people." I have heard about T-shirts that will change the world, edible puffs that will end peanut allergies, stylish eyeglasses made for children, creative storytelling to prevent suicide, and immersive experiences to transform education—the ideas are endless. New ideas emerge every day, but few ideas last. I ask one question to every person who comes to me with an idea: Why are you the person to solve this problem? The reason I ask this question is that I've seen over and over again that the person who connects their ideas to their personal journey will work at a problem until it's solved because it is rooted in their purpose. To bring an idea to life is hard. If an idea is not part of your purpose, it's easy to give up when times get hard, but you can't give up on a purpose.

Jonas Paul Eyewear[3] was started by Laura and Ben Harrison because of the numerous eye surgeries their son endured.[4] It is personal. Love Not Lost[5] is a photography company that began after Ashley Jones lost her daughter Skylar at a very early age and was eternally grateful for the photos given to her by friends.[6] It is personal. Refuge Coffee Co.[7] was imagined when Kitti Murray shared coffee with a refugee friend who claimed this could never happen in their community.[8] Kitti lives in this neighborhood, so it's personal. I could share stories for days about friends who have found purpose through difficult personal experiences. Some of these turning points happen early in life, and others happen after retirement.

Will all these projects last forever? Probably not, but the problems these friends are giving their lives to always point directly back to a reason they should be the ones addressing them. Your purpose will always line up with personal turning points in your life and the difficulties you've endured.

Purpose can be found. Those with the courage to pursue their purpose are hard to find.

Many people can find work, but finding purpose takes courage. I have discovered one very big difference between work and purpose. Work is something that takes us away from our people. Purpose is something encouraged by our people. The people who love us love when we do what we are made to do. The people who love us give us the courage to be the person we are meant to be.

I remember a purpose-filled conversation André and I had on a long road trip. We were talking about my job. André had her feet up on the dashboard, leaning back, sunglasses on as if she was almost asleep.

**I don't think you are doing what you are meant to do.**

Right. I thought you were asleep.

**You're consulting on a bunch of things. But it's like we have pieces of the puzzle, but we haven't put it all together. You just need to jump and do it.**

Yeah, but if I jump, I don't know how I am going to get paid.

**Of course you're scared—everyone is scared before they jump. But you know I don't care about money. I just want you to do what you are supposed to do.**

I get it, but my work is providing stability. Isn't that what you need from me, to be a provider for our family?

**No. I have never needed a provider. What I need is for you to be set free to do the work you were created to do. Even if that looks like instability.**

So you're okay with me not making money?

**Who told you I cared about you making money? What's the worst-case scenario?**

Uh . . . we lose the house?

**Then we lose the house. I make more money than you anyway, so why are you making this such a big deal? If it all fails and you have to get a job, you can go apply at Starbucks. I want our kids to look at our family and care more about how we choose to live than how much money we have. I want our lives to show our kids what matters. When we do what we are made to do, it will show our kids that they can do what they are made to do.**

Are you serious? You really want me to go after this thing?

André pulled her seat up. Took off her glasses and looked at me. Her voice got a bit louder and her face much more serious. I felt like I was in the huddle of the championship game from *Hoosiers*.

**Yes, I am serious about this. You are one of the most unique people I have ever met. You help people do stuff in ways I have never seen before. You are creative. You give courage to people with ideas. You help them make it happen. You connect them to others. I have seen you do it over and over again. Do I know how it's all going to work out? I have no idea. But we have always been given exactly what we've needed when we've needed it. Now, I don't ever want to have this conversation again. We are about more than jobs in this family, and that starts right now. Go do what you are made to do. I'm going to sleep.**

*I still remember every word she said verbatim.*

Sometimes your partner says the exact words you need to hear to move you forward. André was right about my purpose too. I wanted more than to be just a provider. And she was right about making more money than me. This was the moment I needed; her communication and her understanding of my purpose led to a deeper emotional connection between us.

Understanding what you are made to contribute in this world is a process, and that process often involves the affirmation of your partner. I needed to hear from André that she believed in me, that she saw something special in my abilities and would stay with me no matter what happened on that journey. She showed me she wanted me to do what I was made to do. Her gift of courage caused a transformation in my life. It challenged my way of thinking and caused me to ask myself a big question: Did I want the same for her?

## OUR THIRD GREAT LOVE

Our first house had exactly forty-three steps between the front door and the curb of the cul-de-sac. I know this because I counted them every time I lugged in grocery bags from our Honda Accord for three years. Our second house has only four steps. I'm just saying: some decisions are easy to agree on as a couple after a shared hardship.

**Though it wasn't a true hardship, it was real and miserable every single day.**

I remember one evening I came back from the grocery store with every grocery bag hanging off both arms all the way up the forty-three steps.

**Well, at least we got some buff arms.**

I walked into the dining room where you were sitting, and the entire kitchen table was covered with your big fat medical books. I set all the bags on the kitchen counter. Catching my breath, I came over to see what you were studying.

**It was a very important subject.**

This was something I could never undo seeing. When I looked down, I was staring at hundreds of penises. There were easily twelve medical books opened up on the table, each book with photos of human genitalia with the grossest, nastiest outbreaks of sexually transmitted diseases I have ever seen. Those images ruined me.

**We were studying STDs. Gonorrhea. Chlamydia. It's the reality of unprotected sex, and I needed to know them all and see them all to be able to treat this in real life. Very practical.**

Yeah, I might have puked in my mouth.

**Ha-ha. You turned pretty white at that moment.**

I immediately ran out the front door and back down the forty-three steps. I told you to call me when the books were closed. I don't remember where I went, but I knew I couldn't look at those images for one more minute. I was out.

**I see these kinds of things every day at my clinic.**

Let's be honest: it's still very awkward for me to acknowledge that you look at other men's penises every day. And when I realize that many of those things have an STD? It makes me itch a little just thinking about it.

**It's what I do. I'll be honest: your spreadsheets and PowerPoint pitches make me itch.**

That is not the same.

**It is exactly the same. What you do every day sounds dreadful to me, and you wouldn't last five minutes without passing out at my job. We both do work that the other should not do.**

And we have learned to love watching each other do the work we are made to do.

Learning to love the purpose of your partner is one of the greatest gifts you can ever give. But this learning is a process. Even though André and I may be drawn to very different work, we can still be drawn toward each other. Sometimes love has a funny way of bringing two unlikely people with dissimilar passions together in a beautiful way. It is in loving each other, loving what we do, and loving each other's purpose that a lifetime of true partnership is created.

The third great love is our partner's work. Loving the person who is closest to you and encouraging them to do what they are uniquely made to do will change how you live in partnership together. Loving the purpose of your partner creates an instant emotional connection with each other. I don't want to battle against my partner's purpose; I want to celebrate doing purposeful work with my partner.

---

We were invited to play in an indoor coed soccer league. I played soccer in second grade and realized it wasn't the sport for me. André never played soccer in her life but felt like she could because she was Bolivian. We were new to Atlanta and needed to make some friends. So why not?

We were on the same team but had very different abilities. Everyone loved having André on the team because she never stopped running. She was like the Energizer Bunny. I'm still trying to figure out why people liked me on the team—it was probably because I brought André. And I'm a great motivator in any sport—I can pack a mean inspirational hype speech before the game and at halftime.

One game night we showed up about fifteen minutes early to get our shoes on and stretch. We sat on the bleachers right next to the field tying our shoes while watching the end of the game before ours. It was a close game and there was a breakaway. One player against the goalie. His foot went back to kick the game-winning shot, and his foot caught the turf before he even touched the ball. He had so much momentum behind his kick that everyone heard it. The crack. There were probably fifty people in the stands, and forty-nine of them leaned back and covered their eyes, shocked by what they just witnessed. André instantly stood up and sprinted directly to the player who'd fallen to the ground writhing in pain. Everyone else looked away in that moment, but André ran toward the problem. That was a moment when I realized she's made to do the work she does. It doesn't matter if she's at her clinic or not. Her purpose carries her toward those who are hurting.

It was also the first time I discovered I loved seeing André do what she is made to do as much as I love doing what I am made to do.

André has an amazing strength of pushing me in a good way and encouraging things within me that I might not even see in myself. Being in a relationship with her has taught me more about myself than I ever knew before. That car conversation with André opened a new, bigger world to explore my purpose. Her belief in me shifted our dialogue from working to sustain a marriage to reimagining a lifetime of partnership. A lifetime partnership means as we progress together through highs and lows, paychecks and gaps, moments of courage and moments of fear, changing seasons of opportunities and losses—I will support, celebrate, and fight for my partner in her journey of finding her purpose. She was exemplifying a new level of commitment *for* me and a new kind of commitment *with* me.

## FIGHT *FOR* THEM, NOT *WITH* THEM

Have you ever asked whose purpose in your relationship is more important? Warning: (1) This question likely can't be answered definitively, and (2) this question likely will start a fight. It is a controversial question, but it could help clarify some of your priorities. The tension between your competing purposes usually starts with calendar debates and money problems but can eventually lead to heart palpitations and real headaches. Obviously, it's common for couples to compare paychecks, and often priority is given to the larger salary. But this isn't about money: Whose purpose tends to take precedence? Is one more important than the other? Now, you might debate with me on this, and yes, it's unreasonable to compare one human's existence with that of another. But if we are exploring whether we feel our purpose is more important than our partner's, then let's be honest: many of us act like what we do is more important than it really is. That ego is the problem. Resentment creeps into families when the love of one person's work outweighs the love of everyone else.

Throughout this research and in my personal journey, I've needed to remember that overprioritizing work can cause others to question your love for them. This happens more than I care to admit. I believe it is a major tension. If I do work that matters, it can be all-consuming. My attention is focused on the demands of my work. Everything I look at is first filtered through the lens of work. All my decisions are made based on how they will impact my work. I can't go to that game because I have a meeting. I can't go on that trip because I have a big deadline at work. I can't be at that appointment because I'm already booked to go on that work trip. I can't do life because I'm doing work.

There have been moments (months) when my work tainted the joy of my family. I have hurt my kids, and I continually hurt André when I prioritize my own purpose over her purpose and over our love. But if you can love the purpose of your partner with an equal amount of commitment as your own work, you'll be able to create a consistent pattern of responsibility and respect. Supporting your partner's purpose will mean making sacrifices, but reaching a point where all three loves—loving our partner, loving our purpose, and loving our partner's purpose—are working together is crucial to a healthy life. For me, it means I am willing to change my schedule to pick up the kids so André can complete her work. My belief in what she does causes me to take more responsibility for our family and household so she can do her work well.

In our research, only 31 percent of respondents feel encouraged by their partner to pursue their work and dreams. This percentage is way too low. Though we may believe in the abilities of our partners, too many of us fail to provide the support needed to make their dreams a reality.

Do I believe my partner's purpose is equal to my own purpose? Or at the end of the day, do I think my contribution to the world is most valuable? Some questions we don't want to answer, but we still need to consider them. This question targets a core belief defining your relationship.

André literally saves lives every day, and I help people with ideas. Her work is more important for individuals' health, but that doesn't minimize my purpose.

Valuing and even loving our partner's purpose as equal to our own is an example of a new era in "family values." When we love the purpose of our partner, we exemplify for our children a commitment marked by equity, purpose, and partnership. If we want to see more equality in the workplace, I believe the first place we should seek change is in our homes as we evaluate the equity of our partnerships.

It may be unreasonable for you to *like* your partner's work as much as they do. I would need a helmet for every time I passed out seeing the things André sees, does, and fixes. But you can love watching your partner do what they are meant to do. Think about the times you've loved watching your partner do what they are meant to do. Have you gone out of your way to provide extra time for them to do those things? Would you be willing to stay with your kids so your partner can get more schooling? When was the last time you changed your work schedule for your partner's work schedule?

Start watching for those moments when you can minimize your purpose and maximize theirs. Let your ego take a back seat and let their purpose shine.

Now, I want to take a moment to acknowledge that this journey to find meaning in life is more than difficult. The pursuit of purpose can be frustrating, agonizing, and defeating. You may be reading this with doubt that you will ever find your purpose; you may wonder if your partner could ever see your giftings and support them the way you desire. We all have moments of frustration, yet we all have moments of breakthrough too. I want to encourage you to keep trying. Keep asking the people close to you to walk with you on this journey, and don't give up on the pursuit. Even if you and your partner are in different seasons of work, don't be discouraged; there is still hope. We'll dive into those difficult seasons in the next chapter.

## TALK ABOUT IT

Before you move forward, take a moment to answer these questions on your own and invite your partner to discuss them with you.

1. Recount your love story. How do you remember it, and how does your partner remember it?
2. Do you think it is wrong to say you truly love your work? Why or why not?
3. What is one thing you see in your partner that you think is a unique contribution to the world?
4. How do you specifically encourage your partner to pursue their dreams and purpose? How are you being encouraged by your partner to pursue yours? Think about some specific instances that have led to your perspective.

## DO A CHALLENGE

We all need creative ideas for taking what we read and putting it into practice. Share your experience with others and tag @loveorwork #loveorwork.

***Recreate your love story.*** Make a fun presentation of pictures to storyboard it out and remember what happened. If you don't have actual pictures, pull creative images from the internet that can retell your story in a unique way. Remember this challenge is meant to be fun, not perfect (laugh a little). Include a bonus moment of trying to recreate your first kiss.

## LISTEN UP

Add to this journey by listening to a free podcast that relates to this chapter and will give you even more to process. Go to www.loveorwork.com/listenup.

**Charity: Water: Vik and Scott Harrison (Episode 23)**

To be inspired by how one couple joined their purposes together and cofounded an incredible clean water initiative that has brought clean water to 8.5 million people in twenty-six countries, listen to Vik and Scott Harrison share how they found their purpose as creative entrepreneurs. Scott is the *New York Times* bestselling author of the book *Thirst*, and Vik runs the Branded Startup, an organization that supports entrepreneurs with purpose.

Never-Ending seasons of work will lead to unsustainable marriages and families.

-André Shinabarger-
#LoveorWork

CHAPTER 5

# *Seasons of Purpose*

## ANDRÉ

**When you get married you get a second set of eyes. For many people the second set of eyes is a cause of constant tension . . . as opposed to a broader, more expansive view of the world. This other set of eyes is a gift to me.**

—ROB BELL

One day I was asked to play powderpuff football. (Let me also just say, this wasn't high school or college—no, this was as a thirty-year-old woman!) It was a seemingly harmless, hot, sticky summer day in Georgia. About twenty families gathered for BBQ and fun every Memorial Day weekend. There was a huge field, and the male leader thought the men should play flag football. Since the boys' game might be a little too rough, he decided the women should play powderpuff football.

*Ref, I'm taking a thirty-second timeout.*

Before I go any further, can I just ask: what is a powderpuff, and what in the world does it have to do with football? The name itself already insults me. Is this what one calls a girls' touch football game? Don't the men just call it tag or touch football? So let me get this straight: because women are playing, we should add the word "powderpuff"? Dumb it down a little for the ladies?

Here's what I googled: "The name 'powderpuff' originated from the makeup tool that girls would use to powder their faces in public in the 1940s when the games first started, which was more or less a giant fluffy brush."[1] Barf.

No. No, thank you.

Every day women are bombarded with injustices, big and small, that tell us we're weaker than men. Powderpuff = weak. Football = strong. It is exactly the same game that the men play, but women are deceived into thinking we can't play the same game! Before the rules are even explained, we're told it's all puff and powder. This message, and countless others like it delivered by society daily, tells us to move over (or don't move at all) and let the big, burly football player man do the work.

*Thirty-second timeout over.*

So I did what strong women do: I protested. While tradition among this group repeated itself with the same man/woman game breakdown every year, our sons and daughters sat on the sidelines and watched gender-specific games and gender profiling unfold.

I wasn't taking this lightly. I started asking questions to the women around me:

*"Do you think it's weird that we can't play the men's game with them?"*

*"Do you like powderpuff football? Is this the game you really want to play?"*

*"Why can't we play the men's game?"*

These questions stirred the thoughts and imaginations of all the women in the group.

And suddenly the collective wanted a new story.

They wanted to play the same damn game.

And they spoke up. We spoke up.

The collective spoke, and the men listened, and the men's game turned into a coed game for the first time ever. It was a small victory. But I believe history was made in this seemingly insignificant moment. Each and every small moment where women are allowed on the same playing field as men is one step closer to gender equality (and while we're at it—taking down the patriarchy).

When it comes to decisions we need to make together as a couple or as a family, I think these old-fashioned thoughts, these societal norms, have crept into our way of thinking, and as women we unconsciously take the back seat. We let the men go after their dreams and goals, and we hang back and say we will support them. We let the men work, and though we might want a career, we stay home with the kids. We do a thousand other things weekly to keep the family ship afloat, all so the man can "play football" and "win."

Societal norms tell us we *should* do certain tasks deemed as "women's roles" instead of doing the things we love and dream of doing.

*Penalty goes to Society.*

## THE POWER IN POWDERPUFF

One thing I love about Jeff is that he is a fierce feminist. I think growing up in a household with three older sisters helped him out. He has never thought I was less strong; in fact, he has always picked me as his partner in every game and activity we have played. (Not to brag, but we are pickleball champions, indoor soccer champions, and pool volleyball champions to date.) He has never thought I couldn't lead as well as him, and he has often asked me to take the lead in many of our leadership responsibilities. He also has never thought my dreams were less important than his. Society might be sending me messages to be weak and take the back seat, but I know my partner values everything I bring to the driver's seat.

But here is the challenge Jeff and I faced in the first ten years of marriage. We *both* had dreams, and we both wanted to accomplish them. I wanted a career in medicine. Jeff wanted to start a nonprofit. *We both wanted to succeed.* We both wanted to lead and grow and be the best we could be in our work.

*And that was the constant tension. How could we both do that at the same time?*

Medical school is a lot of money and a lot of loans. Starting a nonprofit is a big jump into the unknown of fundraising, financial insecurity, and no health insurance. So we struggled with this dilemma for quite some time and realized we each could go after our dreams—*just not at the same time.*

So I went to medical school, and Jeff stayed at a job that was not ideal so he could support me. Then I got a job, health insurance, and some stability while Jeff plunged into his nonprofit venture. This arrangement worked for us. A seesaw of sorts, a compromise like this requires tension on both ends for it to work.

Maybe your tensions are different. Maybe you want to stay home with your little ones until they are off to school and then get that MBA you always wanted. Maybe you're an empty nester and now you desire to dream creatively about what's next for you. Maybe life feels like an endless sacrifice and you wonder when the time will come for you to dream again. Let's talk about those tensions. Let's air them out in the open and see what our partners think. I can guarantee that if you and your partner care about each other and want the best for each other, then compromises can be made for those dreams to become reality. Everyone and every situation and every tension is different, but we can underscore a few commonalities.

Here are some key principles that have helped us in our dream making:

- Each person has dreams, and each person's dreams matter.
- Pursue all the dreams—one at a time.
- Every season must end.
- When one person is pursuing a dream, the whole family is part of that dream.

Let's get a bit real: I recall a time when one of Jeff's dreams collided with mine.

Jeff's second book was complete, and he was ready to send the final manuscript to the publisher to be printed. The book was called *Yes or No: How Your Everyday Decisions Will Forever Shape Your Life*, a fitting title for the ensuing conversation.

I'm done. I did it! Do you want to read the final version?

**I'm good. I don't really want to read it again. I mean, I've lived all the freaking stories already.**

Wait. What? You don't want to read the final copy of my book? You know I talk about you quite a bit in it. Are you okay with the stories the way I wrote them?

**I mean, at this point I'm okay with whatever. You just need to be done.**

Great. I'm sending it in!

**That's good. I'm happy for you. So, is it my turn now?**

Is it your turn for what? I just finished one of the hardest things I've ever done. How about "I'm really proud of you . . ."

**So, your book is done. Good job. I'm proud of you.**

Thanks?!

**Jeff, you know it's not really done, right? You want to know what happens next?**

Yeah. We go to dinner and celebrate?

**Nope. Next, you release the book. You take extra time for marketing and promoting the book. Then there are the extra interviews and podcasts that you schedule before or after working your real job. Then you have to travel and speak because when you share your story, it sells more books. In short, there is much more to do for this book to actually be done.**

Well, yes. I mean, I do have to work to sell the book.

**Right, and that means more time that you'll be gone. Meanwhile, I have to maintain everything else: kids, school, house, family, and did you remember I have a job?**

I don't really understand. I thought this was what we agreed on. Isn't this what we wanted?

**This is what *you* wanted. And I am supporting you.**

So, you didn't want me to do this? You don't want this book to succeed?

**The problem isn't that I don't want you to succeed. But how does your success impact the entire family? How does the success of this book impact the things I want to do? How long do I have to support you? When does this season end? When is it my turn?**

When is it your turn for what? (I had that sick feeling in

my stomach knowing something was deeply wrong
but I didn't understand what she was saying.)

**When is it ever time for my dreams to happen? When will you choose my dream over yours? When does my purpose take priority? I need for it to be my turn.**

You know and I know he didn't know what he should have known. That is the point. In these magnificent moments of marriage, much more is being communicated than what is actually spoken. In that moment, the space between us was a tightly coiled spring about to pop. That season was focused on Jeff, and I was ready for a shift. It was time for him to relinquish the power of his season and focus attention toward my dreams.

It had been a long year of writing this second book while simultaneously starting his first year full-time at a start-up nonprofit. As any entrepreneur knows, the first year of taking the plunge to work full-time on a start-up is the hardest year, both financially and timewise. We also had two rambunctious children under the age of three. I understood when we started this year that it was going to be tough. Writing a book involves multiple deadlines, and Jeff often needed to get away to organize his thoughts; our lively home didn't provide a quiet, peaceful environment conducive to writing. The year was rough, but I was invested with him and truly hoped for his success. I worked hard to be supportive, hold down the fort at home, and allow him the time and space needed to get away and write. Yet I became increasingly frustrated because the season was far from over and I was ready for a shift in priorities.

Let's be honest: I was tired of carrying the bulk of family and home responsibilities alone. I was tired of every conversation being centered around his book and his work. His rantings usually sounded like the following:

*Will I be able to pay myself this month?*

*Who do I need to meet with about fundraising?*

*How do I find the right board members?*

*This chapter is due next week, and I'm not even close to finishing.*

You see, everything that entire year was all about Jeff's work (and it needed to be). However, when he asked me to read through his book again (since I've always edited every book he has written), I was done. Done talking about his book, done reading the same stories, done with every conversation being centered around Jeff. It was a book titled *Yes or No.* In this moment, I was choosing *no.*

When would my dreams take priority? He'd been at the top of the seesaw while I held down the fort. It was time for a shared shift.

BALANCING WORK AND HOME LIFE

| | ALL COUPLES | MEN | WOMEN | FATHER (KIDS <18) | MOTHERS (KIDS <18) |
|---|---|---|---|---|---|
| WE BOTH PURSUE WORK WE LOVE WITHOUT HAVING TO ALTER OUR HOME LIFE | 27% | 28% | 26% | 20% | 19% |
| FOR BOTH OF US TO WORK, ONE HAS TO HAVE FLEXIBLE HOURS | 23% | 24% | 23% | 28% | 32% |
| WISH I COULD SPEND MORE TIME WITH CHILDREN | 23% | 23% | 23% | 35% | 36% |
| MY SPOUSE HAS SACRIFICED THEIR WORK/ INTERESTS BECAUSE OF MY WORK | 19% | 25% | 13% | 28% | 15% |
| I STAYED AT HOME TO CARE FOR FAMILY SO PARTNER COULD PURSUE WORK/PASSION | 15% | 11% | 19% | 16% | 29% |
| STRUGGLE TO FIGURE HOW TO ACCOMMODATE BOTH OF OUR WORK OR PASSIONS | 15% | 16% | 13% | 18% | 14% |
| PARTNER HAS STAYED HOME FOR FAMILY SO I COULD PURSUE WORK/PASSION | 11% | 17% | 5% | 25% | 7% |
| FOR BOTH OF US TO WORK, ONE HAS TO WORK FROM HOME | 8% | 8% | 8% | 8% | 8% |

Our data indicates that I am not the only person wrestling with this tension. Only 27 percent of couples say they are able to pursue the work they love without having to alter their home life. That means 73 percent of couples have had to adjust in some way.

It's impossible for both of us to balance everything at the same time. One needs to be solid while the other goes after their big dream. One person anchors the seesaw so the other can soar. Then after a period of time (sometimes it can span years, other times weeks), the season must end. And that was the crux of our discussion: I needed the season of holding down the fort (with the crazy kids, dog, school permission slips, and patient needs) to end. I was exhausted and needed some help and needed a chance to soar.

## ONE PURPOSE AT A TIME

Sometimes in this tension between work and love, it simply comes down to a balancing act between who gets priority when. Success as a family unit requires a unified pursuit, and sometimes one dream takes priority over another. In each season we need to ask, at this moment in time, whose purpose is taking priority and whose should take priority? And then reassess the situation regularly.

Our story has been one of shifting between different purposes taking priority at any given time. So how does it work when both people in a committed relationship go all out and pursue their dreams? As exhilarating as that sounds, I have to be honest: it doesn't usually work. I cringe even writing that, but it's true. I really want to say, "Go for it! You can do it!" However, this is one pattern we have observed over and over again that causes marriages and families to disintegrate. Not all, but most.

In any committed relationship there must be seasons when one person takes priority in pursuing their dreams over the other.

This precedence of one partner is not for the totality of their marriage, but seasonal. It needs to be a constant discussion, and societal expectations and gender roles need to be excluded from the equation during this conversation (throw out the powderpuff football and get on the same playing field). It needs to come from a deep place of honesty and humility, believing the best in the other person. Believing that even as I lift my partner to center stage for this season, down the road we'll enter a season when they will do the same for me. Lifting up your partner isn't easy, but it fortifies the fabric of trust. I have been the one supported (medical school) and the one supporting (start-up life), and each season taught me something different and strengthened our marriage and partnership in ways I never could have imagined. Seasons allow us to value each other's service and each other's purpose in the world.

Have you ever heard of an Indo Board? The Indo Board was created in 1998 and was designed to help you improve balance, agility, posture, and stability and to strengthen core muscles—all while having fun (as long as you don't kill yourself in the process). Imagine a pretty flat board that is about 30 inches long and 16 inches wide in the shape of an oval. Under the board is a thick log shape about 6 inches in diameter that rolls left or right. You place the board on the log and try to balance it in the middle without falling off. It's kind of like a one-person teeter-totter where you try to surf in the middle without falling over (I always fall over). You can imagine balancing on the Indo Board is not easy. Left, right, left, right, fall over. Try again and again and again. Except for legit surfers, not many win this game. (Which is why I don't play anymore. I promise I'm not competitive at all.) But I did find a way to win (or maybe cheat). I learned to place the board next to something stable that I could hold on to. It could be a wall or the back of a couch, maybe even the shoulders of a friend. The only way I could actually find balance was to rely on something (or someone) that didn't change or move.

We do this in life, right? We try to find this fictitious ideal called balance. A game of negotiating. If I do this, then can I do that? Left, right. Yet to succeed on this Indo Board, we have to hold on to a third party, this person/thing that stays consistent while we try to find balance. We lean on another, using their equilibrium. While we are engaging a new challenge and figuring out this crazy balance board, we need the stability of a partner standing firmly on solid ground. This image is what I believe we need in our marriage partnerships. One partner must be solid while the other is finding their way.

Now, for fun, let's imagine there are two people on separate Indo Boards (I can tell you this is a very bad idea) trying to find a risky balance in life. Two boards. Two challenges. Two people who are holding on to each other while trying to balance on those wobbly boards. It doesn't work. One leans left and the other leans right. One finds a hint of stability and the other topples over, pulling both of them down into a tangled mess of arms and legs. (I promise I know nothing about this falling into a heap of body parts.)

When Jeff was writing his book and starting a nonprofit, he was all wobbly and wonky on his Indo Board, while I was the person standing on solid ground holding him and the entire family up. The weight I carried felt heavy as I supported everything revolving around Jeff, and I needed to feel like we were on the same team, not just Jeff's team.

## EVERY SEASON MUST END

When Jeff and I had that mammoth fight about his book (aren't you glad you get to be included in all our candid moments?) and the revelation that this book season was all about Team Jeff, the other crucial piece of the discussion was that Team Jeff's season needed to end. Every season, whatever season you are in right now, needs to have a beginning and an end.

My favorite part of the nature cycle are seasons. I love the rhythmic sequence of them. Each season is necessary for life to be sustained. Every season brings an end and a beginning; these are what define a season. The busy growing and harvest seasons are great, but then there has to be rest for the soil. Creation is a beautiful representation and reminder of the truth that our lives too should have seasons.

Why don't we practice seasonal cycles more in our everyday lives?

When you think of the overlapping pursuits of love and work and family and all that those pursuits entail, you may find that seasons are the starting place to make it all work. When we interviewed Tripp and Hannah Crosby, Tripp talked about how each person cannot give every bit of themselves to every area of work, marriage, and family.[2] He asked us to imagine we were given only thirty points to manage every day. Most likely we would never allocate our thirty points evenly—ten for work, ten for marriage, and ten for kids—because *life* doesn't happen that way. You may go through a season when work is super busy, so you allot more points to that area; or when your child is graduating from high school, so you transfer most of your points to helping them through that busy time; or when your partner gets sick, so you apportion points over to them while they are not functioning at their best. This point system needs to be readjusted *for each season*. And that is the key: reminding ourselves regularly that each circumstance that seems frustrating or overwhelming or exhausting is likely only for a season.

If you are running on no sleep and no time for yourself with small kids at home, you are in a season. It will change. Those little ones will grow and begin to wipe their own butts, and suddenly you will be in a new season. (Hallelujah!)

If you are starting a business and not sure if you will be able to pay your bills next month, you are in a season. This too will pass.

If you are juggling teenagers with skyrocketing emotions, you are in a season. One day all those crazy kids will be out of your house as grown adults functioning in society on their own.

There are seasons in your work, seasons in your partner's work, seasons in your marriage, and seasons in each of your kids' lives. The Jeff I married when we were twenty-two is not the same person today. And the same is true for me. I often joke that I have married at least seven different versions of the Jeff I married seventeen years ago. We have walked (and sometimes dragged ourselves) through many seasons that have made us who we are today. Seasons can be long. Seasons can be short. But seasons must have an ending point.

What happens when a season doesn't seem to end? When your partner keeps telling you, "We just have to make it through this busy season," and then it flows into the next busy season, and it never seems to end? What happens then? What happens when a season keeps going on and on and you just can't take it anymore? You feel frustrated, overwhelmed, stuck. Here is the hard truth: you will hit a breaking point, because life cannot be sustained if the season never changes. Just like your body will deteriorate if you only stay awake and never sleep. Yet for some reason we Americans like to hold on to the season of *busy*. Now, don't get me wrong, busy can be good. This season is good. It's needed. We need to work—we need to be productive, get things started, make a difference, change the world. But life is not sustainable if we stay there. Never-ending seasons of work will lead to unsustainable marriages and families. Ruth Haley Barton says, "Most of us are more tired than we know at the soul level. We are teetering on the brink of dangerous exhaustion, and we cannot do anything else until we have gotten some rest."

When Jeff and I discussed his book season coming to an end, he was awakened to my current place of exhaustion. He realized that he needed to stop and step back and help me so I could rest and regroup. This conversation led him to ask me about my dreams. We hadn't talked about those dreams in so long. Life had become too busy. This pause, when he asked and then really listened to me, was the catalyst for my partnership with a clinic in Honduras. Since I had gotten married, gone to PA school, started my first job, and had two babies, I had not been able to stop and dream about anything else outside of this reality. There was no time. Jeff asked me what my dreams were, and I couldn't even give him an answer. So he stopped his book stuff and gave me time. He didn't go on a book tour; he didn't do all the extra promotions. He stayed home. He sacrificially gave me the gift of helping with the house and kids, and he gave me time and space to think and dream. That was one of the best gifts he has ever given me.

In our research, when we asked working couples if they felt encouraged by their partner to pursue their work and dreams, only 31 percent said yes. This stat must change for partners to feel loved and valued and heard in their relationships. Jeff did this for me, so off to Honduras I went, dreaming with a friend who lived and worked there. I collected free medications and supplies, helped train the clinicians in women's health initiatives, and practiced my medical Spanish all over again. My time there was glorious and brought me life and joy. It all happened because my life partner stopped and asked me about my dreams, gave me time and space, and sacrificed his work to make my dream happen. Most importantly, he prioritized me.

## WHEN ONE PURSUES A DREAM, THE FAMILY PURSUES THAT DREAM

One day, we had the opportunity to meet Jeff Foxworthy and his wife, Gregg.[3] Everyone knows that Jeff is the funny guy, but most people have never heard about Gregg or realized that Jeff's career never would have been possible without her commitment to his dream. We were excited to meet them and expected to laugh, but we didn't realize we would soon be inspired to tears. Jeff's first year of touring was difficult. He performed 306 times in one year and was paid $8,000. Total. For the whole year. Let me do the math for you: the average gig paid out about twenty bucks. Gregg had a full-time job and paid all the family bills and, based on this rate, most of the travel bills. She would work Monday through Friday and get on a Greyhound bus (a *bus*—they didn't have enough money for plane tickets) Friday evening to arrive just in time to see Jeff perform in a dingy comedy club. She would sit in the back and take notes in her journal. I loved hearing them share their story. Whenever Jeff spit out a joke and nobody laughed, he would hear her in the back of the club chuckling to herself while taking a note, both of them knowing that joke would not make it into his next set. She did whatever it took for his dream to come to life. She believed in him, supported his dream, and pushed him to do better. His dream became their dream.

Time passed, and as we all know, Jeff's comedy career became wildly successful riding the wave of redneck jokes and hilarious observations of family drama. Meanwhile, he now had two daughters at home. Jeff was determined not to be an absentee father and spouse. Every Friday night, Jeff would do a show and take a red-eye flight to be back home for Saturday morning soccer games with the kids. Then he'd fly back out early evening for his Saturday night show, do his gig, then take a second red-eye flight to be back in time for the family to go to church together Sunday morning. What sacrifice! What commitment!

In one season, Gregg did whatever it took for Jeff's dream. In another season, Jeff did whatever it took for his wife and family.

**Shinabarger, are you thinking the same question I'm thinking? How do you know? How do you know whose dream takes priority? I need your help with this one.**

I think every circumstance is different, André, but there are times when you know one person's momentum is picking up, and I think you should go with it.

**That's good. So the Foxworthys' story is that Jeff kept winning every comedy competition he entered and his momentum was gaining. But the money was not necessarily coming in . . . yet.**

Another question I would ask is: Is the money coming in right now?

**Right, so there are times when your business might be doing really well and the money is coming in, so keep it going! (We also understand that money is not the only factor and it takes time for a business to grow to hit those financial goals.) Also, one partner might have a career where there is only one season in life when they will ever make this much money (sports careers, music, etc.) or even an annual set of months when money comes in (Etsy, retail, etc.), so you should seize that critical and important time.**

Exactly. Also, there are times when you have plenty of money and can think futuristically.

**There are also times when you are not making money, when you are in debt, or when you need to focus on money to get out of a hole.**

We've had those seasons when paying off your school loan was our priority and we both took on extra work just to pay off that debt. We sacrificed with a very tight budget—remember, we didn't even get a Christmas tree that year.

**Yup, it was frivolous, and we couldn't afford anything**

**extra during that time. I remember we chose to live off of your income, and every dollar I brought in went to paying off debt. I think we should also think about mission. Whose project is needed for the betterment of society right now? Is it crucial and relevant to this time and space in history?**

That's good. We just nailed it: momentum, money, mission.

**We did not just do that. An alliteration? Lord, help me. [Eye roll]**

Ha-ha. You won't forget it now. [Fist bump]

Our friends Kyle and Juliet Korver perfectly sum up this question about whose purpose takes priority now.[4] Kyle is an NBA All-Star, and he only has a short period of time (in the big picture of life) when his body will be able to play pro ball. Now, granted, he is one of the oldest players in the NBA (as we are writing this), so his time has lasted much longer than average. As a result, Juliet has had to put a lot of her dreams on hold, move around the country, and single parent most of the season. She also understands that this is his time, his moment to do all he was created to do in the NBA. They both know this season will end—they know he can't be in the NBA forever—but they are setting themselves up for success now so that when he's done, Juliet's dreams will take priority and the family dynamic will shift. They also don't take any of it for granted; Kyle always says that at any time Juliet can have the veto. She can say, "Kyle, I want you to be done." And he will be done with the NBA. He understands all the sacrifices she has made for him to make this dream happen, and he will honor her request at any point in time. Every summer they have an annual off-season time to reassess and edit. "Are we doing this again next year?" Their life is an example of what it looks like when the entire family is part of pursuing the dream.

Getting traded is no joke. It happens quickly, and when it does, the whole family is affected. The house has to be sold. The kids have to change schools. The boxes need to get packed. Yes, we all know as an NBA family they have money and their life is privileged. That isn't the point; the point is that life is altered. On the regular. The kids miss their daddy, communication across time zones is difficult, and often the family feels left behind. His dream, his work, drastically impacts the family and everyone feels it.

Maybe you are thinking, Can I really ask my partner to quit their dream? Isn't that selfish? Isn't that unfair? Won't I feel guilty for that dramatic request?

I understand these tensions, and while appropriate timing is important for ending anything, *it is not selfish to have the discussion together.* It is not selfish to share your hopes and dreams and desires. This dialogue can serve to sweep away lingering bitterness and hurt and replace them with authentic conversation. I want to encourage you to take a brave step toward talking with your partner about when a certain season needs to end. When priorities need to shift. When goals need to be readjusted. If unhappiness or discontent or resentment is growing, this conversation needs to begin.

Negative emotions flag us to problems that need to be addressed. If you are feeling a sense of resentment, discontent, or unhappiness, consider the following questions: Are you and your partner listening to each other's dreams? Are you pursuing too many dreams at once? Has a season gone on too long? Has the family been negatively impacted by a decision you and your partner have made?

Remember these principles: (1) Each person has dreams, and each person's dreams matter. (2) Pursue all the dreams—one at a time. (3) Every season must end. And (4) when one person is pursuing a dream, the whole family is part of the dream. And don't forget that at any time you can edit, readjust, and make changes for the betterment of your marriage, family, and work. This foundation is crucial to ensure that your dual purposes work together to keep you on the same team. We'll talk about that in the next chapter.

## TALK ABOUT IT

Before you move forward, take a moment to answer these questions on your own and invite your partner to discuss them with you.

1. Think back and consider the different seasons that have transpired in your relationship.
2. Are you feeling the tension of one purpose taking priority in your relationship right now? How does that make you feel, and have you communicated this tension with your partner?
3. What do you think about the idea that only one purpose can take priority at a time? Do you agree or disagree, and why?
4. In your relationship, do you feel like a secondary character in the story, or do you feel like you both are on the same team? Without getting into causes or blaming, how could this idea transform your relationship?

## DO A CHALLENGE

We all need creative ideas for taking what we read and putting it into practice. Share your experience with others and tag @loveorwork #loveorwork.

***Recognize that perfect balance is impossible.*** As a way to remind yourself how difficult balance can be, we challenge you to sign up for a yoga class with your partner. You may have never done it before; that's okay (your inexperience will make the class more entertaining). Creating this new experience together will give you a physical reminder of an important principle (and a lot to laugh about later).

## LISTEN UP

Add to this journey by listening to a free podcast that relates to this chapter and will give you even more to process. Go to www.loveorwork.com/listenup.

**Marriage Is Funny: Gregg and Jeff Foxworthy (Episode 25)**

This episode shares Gregg and Jeff's love story and explores how chasing Jeff's dreams of comedy affected their marriage and family. Jeff Foxworthy is a world-renowned comedian and creator of the bestselling game Relative Insanity.

doing LIFE together means choosing your LIFE PARTNER over yourself again and again.

-JEFF SHINABARGER

#LOVE or WORK

CHAPTER 6

# *Same Team*

## JEFF

**Love is a partnership of two unique people who bring out the very best in each other, and who know that even though they are wonderful as individuals, they are even better together.**

—BARBARA CAGE

You go look.

**No, you go look.**

Is it just our debate, or does every couple battle over who should get out of a warm bed to turn off the light or soothe a crying baby at midnight or do whatever it is that means getting cold feet instead of keeping them snuggled under the covers? We have battled over turning off the bathroom light, letting the dog in, and even sneaking tooth fairy money under a kid's pillow.

One time, the season of getting out of bed was a little different and a much more important battle. This battle lasted six months, and it wasn't with each other: it was with a rodent. He would wake us up in the middle of the night. Over and over again. We could hear the little feet scurrying outside the bedroom. In the kitchen, in the living room, in the laundry room, and scrambling across the floor. The entire family named him Ralph the Rat. Ralph was large and thought he was in charge. It was time to show this hairy rodent who was boss.

One of us would get out our phone flashlight and tiptoe out of the bedroom trying not to make a peep. The other would stay in bed waiting for a report.

**I would poke my head out the door and scan the room with the light, trying to spot him. One time I got a glimpse of the beast before it scurried off. "Holy crap! He is huge! I think he's a raccoon, not a rat!"**

We tried everything. We got the sticky traps. We got the snapping traps.

**We called the exterminators. They enclosed the house and set up traps everywhere.**

Now the rat was stuck in our house! I didn't have another good night's sleep. Nope. I was not okay with this plan.

**We would hear the scampering every night.**

Every night we could hear Ralph. Every morning we saw the effects of Ralph. But we could never catch Ralph.

**Ralph became part of the family. It was kind of like Elf on the Shelf.**

Um, no, never part of the family. Every morning the kids would wake up curious to see what mischief Ralph got into the night before.

**He ate through a cushion on our couch. He gnawed through a backpack just to find a granola bar. He would leave apples half-eaten on the counter. One night he even ate an entire bag of sweet potato chips in one sitting. Ralph was destroying everything in the house. It was time to devise a plan.**

I can't even eat a whole bag of chips in one sitting! But we knew he liked sweet potato chips . . . so it got us thinking.

**I mean, who doesn't like sweet potato chips?**

We had our bait. It was time to regain control of our house.

**Every night, we would make a line of sweet potato chips leading into a metal rat trap that would close and catch him alive.**

Every night—we set up the trap right on our kitchen counter. And we waited and waited . . .

**We had a plan. We were going to win this battle. We were in this together. Then . . . *snap!* I woke up immediately. "We got Ralph!"**

"Are you sure? You go check."

**"I'm not going to check that trap. We need to call the exterminator." It was in that moment I realized that we actually were not on the same team.**

We were on the same team, and as my teammate, you needed to get rid of it.

**We got him. All ten inches of him plus his foot-long tail. Ralph was done.**

Sometimes shared experiences bring us together as a couple

in a way we can't fully explain. The problem is that too often our projects separate the two of us instead of uniting us. It's because of this that we have to be proactive about creating experiences that unite us.

Shared experiences begin with prioritizing time and space for your partner. We need to prioritize caring for each other before we care for our kids, or our not-so-much pet rat, or our own warm feet.

## CLEAR THE NOISE

Have you ever been in a large room with acoustic problems? Every sound wave bounces incorrectly, amplifying everything else. It makes you talk louder, but no one can hear any better. Instead, everything grows louder and louder and louder. Soon the noise becomes deafening. In our house it sounds something like this: André starts playing music through the kitchen speaker while cooking dinner. Neko flies through the house on his roller skates from the front door to the back over and over again (falling and flailing over and over again). Our dog, Josie, starts barking and chasing Neko, thinking this is a fun game. Jada is trying to finish her homework and starts yelling at Neko and Josie to be quiet. I turn up the volume of my basketball game because I can't hear over the music, skating, barking, and yelling. André yells at me because the TV is too loud and she can't hear her music. She turns up her music. All noise, no listening. Have you felt these moments of audible insanity too?

We all want attention, and the noise plays well beyond audible insanity. Consider the constant communication noise that fills our lives: calendar requests, instant message notifications, urgent emails, red dots on your phone, alerts, recordings, voicemails, news updates. As more noises in our lives demand attention, we end up giving the most attention to the loudest ones, even when those are the least important.

Why do we let the push notifications compete with the voices of the people who matter most?

When your partner's voice gets drowned out, or there's just not enough time for their voice in between the sounds of work and kids, a chasm opens up. And the longer the silence, the wider the chasm grows. Maybe you find yourself working sixty to eighty hours per week for weeks on end, and when you *are* home, you're not fully present because work is a noisy distraction. Maybe on weekends you and your partner are busy separately carting kids from one soccer game to the next. All play for the kids, a day of disconnection for you and your partner. Maybe your partner isn't sleeping because the baby isn't sleeping and is too exhausted to hang out at night. Maybe you have separate friend groups and it feels like you don't see each other as much as you would like. Maybe you struggle to find time to reflect on what you're actually feeling. Maybe your partner keeps asking you to put your phone down. Maybe your house is a mess and you haven't cooked a meal all week. Maybe we all understand this way too much. And maybe we need to recognize how all these little things create a gulf of silence. Closing the distance between you and your partner will take work, and it can only happen when you tune in to their voice.

When you prioritize your partner and the need to hear their voice, you are in the right place to pursue your work with the support of your family. Whose voice are you choosing to listen to? Without proactive attention to your life partner and your family, the bitterness of being muted will trickle into life like a leaky faucet.

## USE A SHARED CALENDAR

Listening to each other begins by planning your time together. Time management is one of the greatest struggles for families. The tension is not so much *if* you can have it all but *how* you will make it all happen in the hours you have available. And maybe more importantly, how do your hours line up with your partner's hours?

A shared plan is crucial. Only 25 percent of the people we surveyed said they worked together to set a plan, vision, or goals for their year. So three out of every four couples have no plan for where they are going together. I can imagine these couples experience a sense of confusion or a lack of shared vision from a long-term planning perspective. Meanwhile, only 31 percent of the people we surveyed use a shared calendar as a family. This may lead to gaps in the daily understanding of what is happening next, who is doing what, and where everyone needs to go. Without a clear understanding of schedules and priorities, family members will encounter endless unmet expectations and missed opportunities to connect with one another.

Personally, if André and I didn't plan together, we would constantly be frustrating each other. If we didn't have a shared calendar, we would constantly be missing each other. If we didn't have a vision for being together, there's a good chance we couldn't stay together. Planning together and using a shared calendar play vital roles in keeping us together.

When two people in a relationship are doing meaningful work, there will be clashes in scheduling that cause a debate between two good things. In our situation: my good thing and her good thing. These two competing good things have the ability to cause one big conflict.

At some point all the things competing for our time compete for our priority and love too. Saying yes to good things doesn't always equal a good decision for your partner or family. Good things start out competing for your own time, but ultimately they compete with time you could be spending with your partner and family. Good things competing with good things. It's a slippery slope if you both get comfortable filling your time with "good things" that aren't done together.

*You go to that board meeting, and I'll stay with the kids.*

*I'm going to this work dinner, and you go to that game.*

*You do this good thing, and I'll do that good thing.*

*Let's get a babysitter, and you go to that fundraiser while I go help our friends pack up their house.*

We start doing a bunch of good things but miss doing good things together. It turns out that doing good things without prioritizing time for your partner and their good things isn't good after all.

So if you want to start making life easier for you and your partner, make a shared calendar. If you are one of the 69 percent who don't have a shared calendar, please stop right here. I need you to make a joint calendar with your partner before you read one more page. It could be a Google calendar on your phone, a whiteboard calendar in the kitchen, a paper calendar that is open on the counter. *Any kind of calendar.* But please stop and make one now. It may take some time to get both of you using it and working together on it, but give it a try. You and your spouse will be happier, I guarantee it.

## PRIORITIZE TIME FOR YOUR PARTNER

Earlier I asked, how do you choose between two good things? The answer that has always worked for us: *choose each other first.* Whenever we are connected and sharing life together, our decision-making happens more easily and doesn't feel as competitive. When we prioritize each other, our collective priorities become more obvious to each other.

The following ideas are not rocket science; they're simple marriage hacks that help make life run a little more smoothly with more space for listening and love. When implemented proactively, they ease the tension of love and work.

***Go on consistent dates.*** The greatest advice I can give to a working couple is simply to create a standing date night. This idea might not sound remarkable or revolutionary. It's not. But when you create consistent times for each other, the chances of you staying together in a committed relationship are simply greater. At a minimum, you should go on a date once a month, but ideally once a week. Now, if you don't have a shared calendar, planning a date night will be difficult. So look ahead on a calendar and pick a night. A date is a set time and space where you can listen, talk, and connect on big and small things in big and small ways.

If you are not prioritizing dates because of money, consider reaching out to another couple with whom you can trade off babysitting nights to make it happen. Try it once with some friends and see how it goes.

Then get creative. Take turns planning the date. We have created a resource to help you with planning dates. You can download it at www.loveorwork.com/creativedates.

Scheduling date nights on a calendar strengthens a "same team" mindset, and the benefits will trickle into everyday life. When you and your partner are not on the same team, everyone in the house will feel your frustrations. If the two of you are at odds, the whole family will suffer. Special time designed for each other, with each other, will result in better, more committed time spent with everyone else.

***Ask curious questions.*** Something I always try to bring with me on a date is at least one question we can talk about. One is a must, but you can up the ante with a handful of them. These questions are meant to help you dig deep together. A good question stops you from using time together to talk logistics of work or family life and instead gets you to explore each other's thoughts, beliefs, wonderings, ambitions, souls, and fantasies in new and different ways. If you struggle coming up with next-level questions, we recommend downloading the Gottman Institute's app[1] that readies your phone with a variety of curiosities to explore. If paper copies are more your jam, check out the flip book[2] from The Known Project[3] or order a deck of questions from Defy Drift.[4] There are countless resources you can take on a date to stir up quality conversation leading to greater connectivity. The more you talk deeply with each other, the more your interest and intrigue will grow.

***Do proactive counseling.*** According to relationship and marriage expert Dr. John Gottman, couples wait an average of six years of being unhappy before getting help.[5] We waited sixteen years before we went to marriage counseling for the first time (which we do not recommend). We needed some mediation as we navigated starting this new project centered around marriage. We didn't want our Love or Work project to negatively impact our partnership. Proactive counseling is the most common need for couples, yet only a small percentage of couples actually use this helpful resource in marriage. In our research, only 8 percent of couples were actively engaged in counseling as a couple. Though *you* may be interested in counseling, your partner may not. If I'm honest, I really didn't want to go to counseling. The story I told myself was that André wanted to go to counseling because there was some big issue she wanted to bring up, and that scared me. I needed to overcome my own fear of failure to draw closer to her. If your partner doesn't want to join you, try it out for yourself. Individual counseling sessions to help you heal from past trauma or unpack issues regarding family of origin can be extremely beneficial. Both individual counseling and couples counseling have tremendous value.

Our research findings highlight the three most important actions couples can take together to help ease the tension between love and work and to help a relationship thrive: (1) Schedule consistent dates. (2) Through intentional question asking, continually be curious about your partner and with your partner as you continue to grow as individuals. And (3) start marriage counseling sooner rather than later. These three actions, when prioritized and done consistently and authentically, will help solidify your partnership as you do life together on the same team.

## A DIFFERENT APPROACH TO TEAMWORK

Being on the same team means being a good listener. You cannot silence your partner—ever. Teammates depend on each other. Failing to listen or be present shifts the energy in a "same team" mentality. Often when the energy between us is off, when one of us feels unheard or unsupported, we have to restate our mantra to each other: *we are on the same team.* We literally say it out loud to each other almost every week—sometimes in the middle of an argument. It's just a phrase, but it's a reminder to both of us—we are off kilter and we need to reset. It keeps us away from a negative dialogue in our heads that spirals into me against you or you against me. It reminds us in the midst of tension that we can ease it with a quick timeout and reminder: Hey, you and me. We're on the same team.

Why am I cleaning the kitchen again? *Same team.*

Why am I the only one who cleans the bathroom? *Same team.*

Why am I always paying all the bills? *Same team.*

Why does she get so much free time when I'm always working? *Same team.*

When I'm in a one-sided mindset, I forget. I start looking at our marriage and responsibilities as a scorecard. It becomes about what *I* have done. It becomes *my* team. Technical foul. Nobody wins when we create a scorecard for a blame game. Anytime we blame the other person, there's a good chance we're not on the same team. I forget she wants to support and help me just as I want to do the same for her. Just as any teammate would. Then I remember how she folded all the laundry, how she made lunches and dropped the kids off at school the last three days in a row. I remember the countless ways we work on the same team every day.

---

Meet Tedashii[6] and his wife, Danielle.[7] Tedashii is an artist and rapper, and Danielle is a wellness coach and yoga instructor. Tedashii's growing influence has led to the need for him to be on the road touring and for Danielle to take greater responsibility for their children. We had dinner with them, and Tedashii explained the idea of being on the same team further. "I always thought we were on the same team. But really, I was the quarterback and she was the wide receiver." In other words, he was driving the team and she was supposed to respond to whatever he threw at her. Tedashii realized he needed to change his view of "same team." He really didn't understand the impact on their relationship when he didn't take time to listen to her needs and the needs of the family. I see this play out in so many relationships. Too often one person guides all the people toward a place that benefits only that one person. I resonate deeply with the quarterback concept. Too often my priorities take the lead. Too often I act like the QB of my own team. That's not how I want it to work, but the reality is that my actions point to a "Jeff's team" mindset, not to a same team viewpoint.

This team is not only my team; we are on a team together. Repeat it out loud with your partner: *we are on the same team.*

## SAME TEAM MEANS FEELINGS MATTER

Being on the same team means we freely share feelings. Let me give you permission to tell your spouse whatever you feel about this season. Not sharing how you feel actually shows you don't believe you and your partner are on the same team. When we're on the same team, *each* person's feelings matter, whether they are positive or negative.

Other times we need to stop and reassess by asking our partner, "What do you need from me for us to feel like we are on the same team?" When we ask this question of each other, the spiral of negativity stops. It's funny how one statement can turn into a reset for us. Same team reminds us we are not doing life in competition; instead, we are choosing a life of togetherness.

What worked last week, last month, or last year might not work now. Changes in family dynamics, work schedules, and combined priorities require consistent evaluation of what it means to be on the same team.

We learned this in our interview with Steve and Sarah Dubbeldam,[8] co-creators of the magazines and media companies Wilderness[9] and Darling.[10] They shared how sometimes one week might lean more toward "Team Steve" and the next week might angle more toward "Team Sarah." They need to communicate with each other when life feels off. They feel the freedom to call out the obvious lack of balance, especially when one person is cruising along in their own lane and not giving much thought to the joint effort of family life. For the Dubbeldams, gently calling each other out has become a lighthearted way to create a consistent check-in for both partners. There will be times when one person's priorities are impacting everyone's priorities, but it's important to call out those moments to bring back the balance moving forward.

## SAME TEAM MEANS SAME SIDE

Think about the last fight you had with the person you love. You were probably sitting across from your partner, pointing, maybe yelling. It was as if you were on two sides of a volleyball net. Two different teams. A divide between you. Me versus you. A battle of who will win. Too often we approach disagreements this way. Instead of "same team," we are competing for the win.

Joy and Billy Phenix[11] were the first to introduce us to the "whiteboard conversation," a way to see things from the same side instead of from opposite sides of the table. They have a literal whiteboard in their house and use it for disagreements. It seems kind of funny to use a business approach for a family partnership, but it works. Sit in a room. Sit in two seats next to each other and write your problem on the whiteboard. The whiteboard becomes a third party. The actual physical process helps: get on the same side, sit next to each other (which automatically defuses any escalating emotions), and write the problem down. You can write pros and cons lists. You can write what each person thinks and see where there are commonalities and differences. You can draw a plan for how to move forward. When we stop taking sides and write the problem together on a whiteboard, we increase our chances of coming to a resolution together. Instead of thinking, "How can I change your mind?" we ask, "How can we fix this together?" Doing life together inevitably involves conflict, but addressing the conflict in collaboration—not competition—will lead to same team problem solving.

## SAME TEAM MEANS CLEAN AGREEMENTS

We learned another great tip from Jeanne and Jarrett Stevens,[12] cofounders of Soul City Church in Chicago, that is a great follow-up to the whiteboard conversation. In their work together coleading a community, they found that their sticking point wasn't whether they could agree on something but what happened *after* that agreement. So they came up with the phrase "clean agreements" to describe their process of clearly articulating what is going to happen, who is going to do it, and when it will get done. What, who, and when. It's an easy communication tool to get both partners on the same page. This is one of those tools that seems obvious but that doesn't happen nearly enough. What usually happens in our house is that when André asks me to do something, her expectation is that I will do it immediately, if not sooner. But in reality, I'm already doing something else, and therefore her request is not my top priority. Then I forget to do it, and she gets frustrated that I didn't get it done. (Anyone else feel the tension?) If at the beginning we had stopped and communicated our "clean agreement"—what needs to get done, who will do it, and when—we both could have avoided frustration. Clean agreements make life easier (and guarantee less fighting).

## SAME TEAM MEANS NO SECRETS

Secrets are rarely secret. Secrets will never, I repeat, never stay secret. Every time I think I'm keeping a secret from André, she usually already knows something is going on. We try to hide things, but they are always found. We have past failures we try to tuck away, deeming them unimportant to the present. Being on the same team gives us an opportunity to share our secrets and accept our own and our partner's failures with love and grace instead of hiding and retreating. In an age of social distancing, sometimes we try to distance the truth from the people we care about, causing secret lives and untold stories.

When we interviewed our friends Tripp and Hannah Crosby, they shared their rule about not having secrets as a couple. Their commitment has set a new tone for our relationship and is very important in every relationship. If they mess something up (and we will all mess something up), they talk about it. More grace and honesty with less shame and hiding. No matter what the topic, they share openly, and sometimes that honesty hurts each other. But it would be better to be honest and hurtful than hiding and broken. I know Tripp is even transparent with Hannah about his internet history and his scary dreams. Sometimes transparency can lead to tears, and other times it leads to overcoming fears, but usually ends with deeper connection. They love each other even in the midst of failures and embarrassing truths. When you experience honesty, even when it hurts, there is an opportunity for kinship that enhances commitment. This thought is embodied in the words of Fred Rogers: "Love isn't a state of perfect caring. It is an active noun like struggle. To love someone is to strive to accept that person exactly the way he or she is, right here and now."[13] Sometimes success in a relationship is the safety of our relationship—rooted in honesty, watered with grace. Let's not have secret passwords. Let's not have secret messages. Let's not have secret lives. No secrets. We will all make mistakes in our relationships. We will all do things we wish we didn't do. We all need a safe relationship in which we can share our full selves with the belief that our partners will reciprocate with love. Same team.

## BETTER TOGETHER

If you're like me, at the end of every day, you *know* whether you and your partner went through that day on the same team. As you are reading this chapter, you know it too. We all know that not every day will be a "same team" kind of day. That's why we all need consistent check-ins to bring us together again and again and again. The best way to begin is to start naming the obvious. Get back to the things that have always drawn you close. Sometimes repeating a simple catchphrase can help unite you and your partner. Sometimes sharing your schedules will bring clarity to each other. Sometimes going on a date will remind you that you love each other. Sometimes just being curious about your partner's life will remind your partner that you care. Sometimes you need to share a secret and your partner needs to respond with grace. "Same team" is not meant to be a nagging philosophy; it is meant to be a unifying mentality to bring couples back together. Doing life together means choosing your life partner over yourself again and again. Staying committed to your partner will mean making daily choices to deny yourself and do life with this other special person, even when life is hard. In the next chapter, André will share about one of her hardest seasons when she experienced both depression and burnout.

## TALK ABOUT IT

Before you move forward, take a moment to answer these questions on your own and invite your partner to discuss them with you.

1. Sometimes we need to reassess and ask our partner, "What do you need from me for us to feel like we are on the same team?"
2. Think about a time when you and your partner worked together to accomplish a shared goal. How did that experience bring the two of you closer together?
3. Do you feel a sense of competition in any aspects of your partnership? What does "same team" mean to you?

4. Are there currently secrets in your relationship that need to be shared? How can you create a safe place to be honest with each other? Commit to being open and vulnerable.

## DO A CHALLENGE

We all need creative ideas for taking what we read and putting it into practice. Share your experience with others and tag @loveorwork #loveorwork.

***Whiteboard your life.*** Sit next to your partner and identify a tension you keep experiencing in your relationship. Or draw out a challenge you are facing as a family. Work on it together on the whiteboard and find a solution together.

## LISTEN UP

Add to this journey by listening to a free podcast that relates to this chapter and will give you even more to process. Go to www.loveorwork.com/listenup.

### Mental Health and Living without Secrets: Tripp and Hannah Crosby (Episode 34)

Listen to this podcast if you want to hear a vulnerable conversation about a marriage without any secrets. Hannah and Tripp are both advocates for counseling and share the importance it has played in their personal lives and marriage. Tripp is a comedian and filmmaker, and Hannah is an abstract artist.

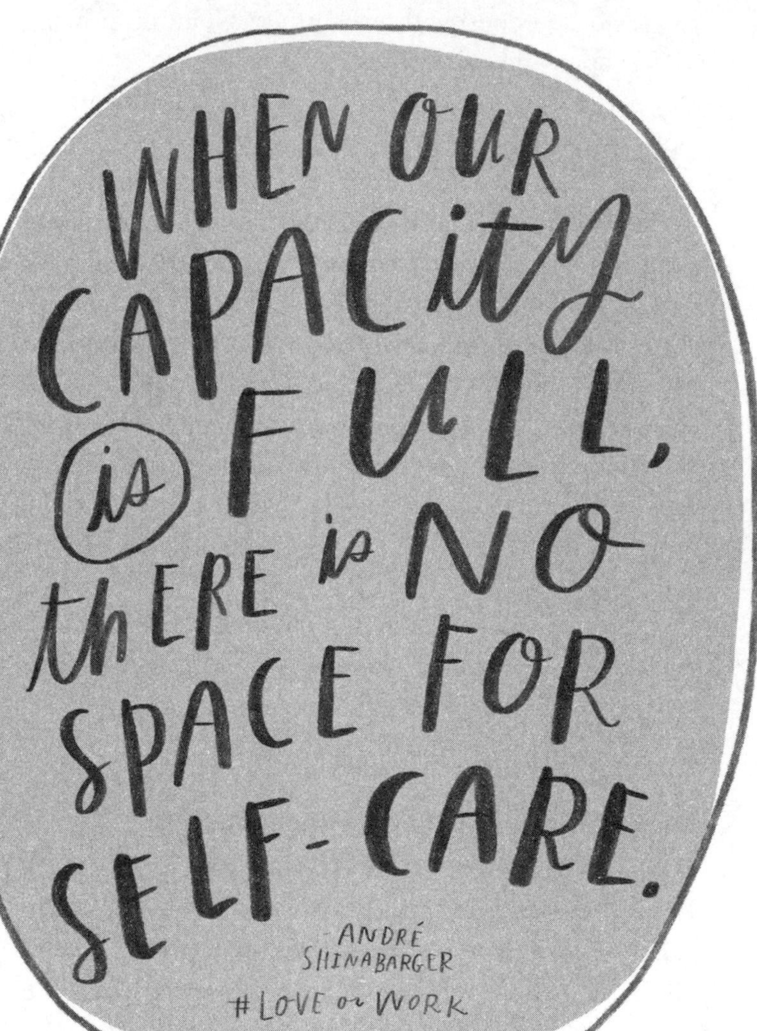
WHEN OUR
CAPACITY
is FULL,
there is NO
SPACE FOR
SELF-CARE.
-ANDRÉ
SHINABARGER
#LOVE or WORK

CHAPTER 7

# *Care and Capacity*

## ANDRÉ

**We had entered an era of limitlessness, or the illusion thereof, and this in itself is a sort of wonder. . . It would take me years of reading, thought, and experience to learn again that in this world limits are not only inescapable but indispensable.**

—WENDELL BERRY

**You need to check me into a mental institute.**

Wow. Really? Let's take a deep breath and talk about that.

**Take a breath? I wake up at 5:00 a.m. to train. I get ready, get Jada ready, and drop her off. I work till 6:00 p.m. Pick up Jada and make dinner. We play, put her to bed, and then I have charts to finish. Also, I have to make a cake for my nurse's birthday tomorrow! And! And! I have nursery duty on Sunday!**

First of all, you don't make cakes, you bake cakes. Second of all, you don't even know how to bake.

**Is that what you got out of all the things I have on my plate right now?**

Okay, okay. I'm sorry, you're right. You are juggling many things. So what can I do to help?

**[Sigh] Well, you definitely need to bake the cake. You're way better at that than I am.**

Got it. What else do you need?

**I don't know what I need, but I feel like I'm dying inside.**

What do you mean?

**I am working all these hours, yet I still can't catch up, so I feel like I should work more. Then I come home and try to be a good mom to Jada, but I'm so tired, yet I should be a happier mom for her. Then you come home and I should want to hang out with you, but I fall asleep.**

André, you're putting too much pressure on yourself. All these "shoulds" that are impossible.

**I know. I know. I just can't keep it all together. Something has to give.**

Okay, so if you could have a break right now, what would you do?

**I'd take a nap.**

Okay, we can make sure you get a nap. What else?

**I need a break, a long break from work. I can't do it anymore. See, if you check me into a mental institute, I don't have to go to work.**

Ha-ha. Okay, so let me get this straight: the inpatient center will keep you from work.

**Exactly! [Hands thrown in the air]**

Listen, everyone has their limits, and I think you've reached yours. So how about this: you go take a nap, and we'll talk more later. [Said in his most soothing voice]

Sometimes our partner knows what we need more than we do. (And also, thank God for the sane one in our relationship.)

When I hear the word *limitation*, I kinda cringe. It feels like a brick wall with no way through. A hard stop. We've all heard the inspirational one-liners telling us, "Sure, you can bust through that brick wall":

*The sky's the limit!*

*You can do anything you set your mind to!*

*You have infinite potential!*

This backdrop of a world with endless potential is the picture we paint for ourselves and for our kids. We don't want to say we can't do something. We want access to all things. Yet life decided to show me something about this word, and it was akin to walking into a brick wall.

There was a long period of time when my work was crazy. The "understaffed" kind of crazy. We usually had eight doctors on staff, but we were down to two doctors and me running the urban health center. We had too many patients with too many needs and not enough person-power to handle the workload. Vacation was restricted. It was common in those days to stare bleary-eyed at my computer screen until midnight while Jeff slept peacefully on the couch next to me. I was so overwhelmed I could barely sleep. My restless nights included dreams about patients dying. Sometimes I dreamed I missed an important finding that inevitably led to the death of a patient. I developed feelings of helplessness and loss of control. The burnout that led to the depression was gradual. I dreaded going to work. I would cry myself to sleep for no specific reason. I didn't want to talk to Jeff (he was dealing with so much already) or to my family, and I avoided close friends at all costs. Life felt very dark and very lonely. I completely understood Parker Palmer's description: "Depression is the ultimate state of disconnection. . . It deprives one of the relatedness that is the lifeline of every living being."[1]

A few months into this ultimate state of disconnection, I was required to attend a medical conference and hoped some time away from the office would help lift my mood. While strolling through the convention center, I got lost looking for a specific class on heart failure and wandered into a small session where an old Native American man was teaching about burnout signs and symptoms. I stared at the PowerPoint presentation and the twelve symptoms listed and realized I had every one of them.

The hour went by in a blur as I sat in shock with tears running down my face. I was astonished by the happenstance that led me into this room at this time to hear this message. For the first time in six months, the fog over my mind lifted and I felt clarity: I was experiencing actual, bona fide burnout. As the session ended and I scrambled to keep my head down, blow my snotty nose, and grab my things, a hand fell on my shoulder. I looked up into his brown face, his eyes kind with understanding. "I've been there," he said. He handed me a small book and said, "Maybe this will help."[2]

I devoured the book that night and came home feeling lighter than I had in months. Something needed to change. Sometimes the greatest gift we can receive is simply the right words to describe what we feel when we are lost in hopelessness. I needed to hear my "diagnosis" so I could figure out a way to heal. I was fatigued, downtrodden, overworked, and still felt like everything I did was never enough. I needed to find a new, healthier way of living.

Parents today are very positive about love and work, yet when we peel back the feelings about the concept, the research tells a different story. Fifty-two percent of women with kids under age eighteen are exhausted. Forty-five percent are overwhelmed. And 28 percent experience guilt (due to working and raising children). Men vary slightly, with 41 percent reporting they are exhausted, 28 percent saying they are overwhelmed, and 10 percent saying they feel guilt. While optimism about love and work seems to guide the everyday motions of doing both, research shows that at the end of the day, 46 percent of working parents are drained. With nearly half of all working couples with children feeling worn out, I wasn't alone in my own plight of exhaustion. These findings also warrant a deeper exploration because working couples with children are not living healthy lives if nearly half are feeling run-down.

NEGATIVE FEELINGS ABOUT WORKING AND PARENTING

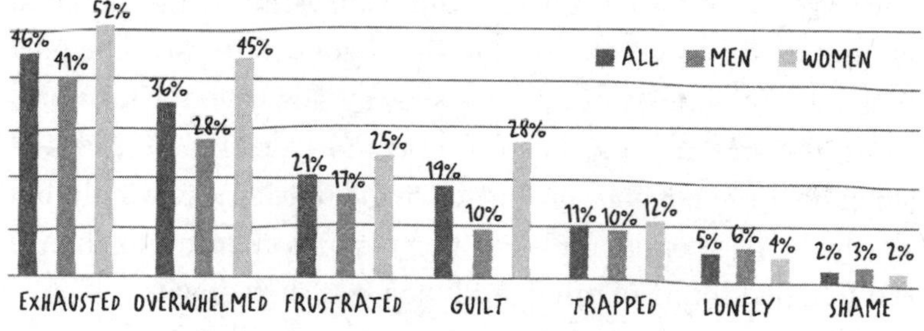


Given all the responsibilities and demands in the balancing act of love and work that we call life, how do we find rest? How do we find time to care for ourselves? Our research indicates a fundamental need to reflect inward to understand how the "busy" in our lives is directly correlated to our choices and actions.

I didn't know what the next step should be to help my burnout, but maybe the mental institute wasn't the right choice at the time. I was very ready to start some antidepressants and get my butt to therapy, but I also needed to take a break from work for a period of time. Work was my trigger and part of the source of my misery at the time. So Jeff and I chose to start with taking a long break and planned to take the next steps when we returned.

A few months later we flew off to Nicaragua with our eighteen-month-old daughter for a three-month sabbatical. In this rest, everything changed for our family.

We started our sabbatical at an eco-lodge in the middle of a coffee plantation in the mountains. Think: the middle of nowhere, with really good coffee. The eco-lodge was *very eco*, so when it was dark, it was dark. The darkness invited more sleep than we'd ever slept. We rose with the sun and slept when it set. That's right, tucked in by 7:00 p.m. It was dreamy. We were off the grid and forced to join the rhythms of Mother Earth.

It was on Mother Earth's daily schedule when we first realized we were missing some major natural rhythms in our love-and-work pace back home. We missed true rest and we missed true play. We missed a lot of sweet moments of noticing the good around us. So much is missed in the chaos of survival. The poet Atticus once said, "It always pays to dwell slowly on the beautiful things . . . and the more beautiful the more slowly." This idea of stopping the chaos and slowing down did not come naturally, but slowly the pace of life on the coffee plantation began to change our frenzied frame of mind, and the noise died down.

## LET GO

The coffee plantation started our journey of slowing down, but I soon realized there was more to untangle. The biggest issue: I had a serious control problem. Part of this control is a survival strategy to keep the peace and keep life moving. Control keeps us safe and efficient. Control = success (society says). But what does that do to a marriage? What does that do to our children?

Can one have control over everything and exude the compassion and care that are necessary to let love grow? This strong iron grip of control made me want to do it all and do it all the "right way" (whatever that means). When we try to control others, nobody wins.

How could my partner, my kids, and my friends feel free to make mistakes, to grow, to learn in their own ways, when I kept clinging to the notion that everything had to be done right, done the way I wanted? The more time we spent with nature, the more I realized the loud distraction of my need for control and the way my actions didn't match my real wants for my family. I was contorting my life into the perfect, gets-all-the-likes Instagram picture I imagined, but in reality, the image needed editing to be the picture-perfect one for all to see.

I was clinging tightly to a life that only suffocated others and prolonged this season of burnout in an unnatural way. I failed to see that even in this season of darkness there could be a light of becoming who I was supposed to be. Do we view our hard times as a gift, a season to learn and grow? Parker Palmer eloquently says, "The notion that our lives are like the eternal cycle of the seasons does not deny the struggle or the joy, the loss or the gain, the darkness or the light, but encourages us to embrace it all—and to find in all of it opportunities for growth."[3]

I gained this fresh mindset after interviewing Katherine and Jay Wolf,[4] coauthors of *Hope Heals*.[5] Katherine suffered a major brain stem stroke at the age of twenty-six, in their first few years of marriage after having their first child. Suddenly their ideal picture of marriage, family, and work was snatched away. Jay became a caretaker, and Katherine became a mother and wife with a disability. They now work to help others understand that *hope is not the opposite of hurt*. They shared that suffering is hard and painful yet also beautiful and good. It can all coexist. She said, "If hope is rooted in an outcome, then your expectations will crush you." This amazing woman was suddenly and unexpectedly handed a different life, full of hardships, and she taught me that all of it, the dark and the light, became integral to her healing.

I think we all have junk in our past and present that we want to hide. May we all realize that the darkness, the burnout, the loud noises do not need to be edited from our picture; they need to be stewarded into our healing.

## WHO YOU ARE NOT

While we were in Nicaragua, Jeff was writing his first book, *More or Less*, and I had no job or specific purpose besides spending time away for my healing and for my family. We met many travelers along the way, and the Americans always seemed surprised by this concept of not working.

"You mean you're not doing any volunteer work? No mission work? No job?"

"Nope, I'm just here for vacation with my family."

The Europeans, however, needed no further explanation. They would laugh and say, "Us too! Isn't it wonderful here?" I love the Europeans. They know what it means to take a holiday.

*This* is America's identity problem.

I remember struggling with telling people I wasn't there for any definitive purpose. I wanted to lie and make something up. I wanted to find an organization that needed some medical help and jump in, feel useful. Then the thought would exhaust me, and I would let it go, take a deep breath, and realize that this was just what it was: lazy American me on a nice long vacation. But was that really it? Why did I want to lie so bad? That's when I realized my identity was intertwined with my job. Suddenly, without my job, I felt exposed and not good enough.

Maybe you have also realized your identity is bound up in something you do. You unexpectedly lose your job, you go on maternity leave, you are in transition between careers, you go back to school, your kids leave for college. Have you felt that deep sense of insecurity and asked yourself, "Who am I?" and "Am I enough?"

Maybe your identity is not just connected to what you do; maybe it's connected to someone you imagined yourself being, but it hasn't happened. Maybe you imagined yourself as a mother, but instead you have struggled with infertility. Maybe you imagined being married for life, but instead you are divorced and starting over. Maybe you imagined your kids outliving you, but instead you are grieving the death of a child. Maybe you have just become an empty nester, and you can't imagine what life will look like now that your parental responsibilities have diminished. You have a new story you never imagined. You have lost something that is so deeply a part of you; grieve that first. And then let me encourage you with this: that is one component of you, but it is not *all* of you. There is so much *more* to you.

There is a gift in feeling lost. The wandering and questioning and suffering can lead to a beautiful self-discovery through which we become whole and true to ourselves. Richard Rohr writes, "God seems to send us on a path toward our own wholeness not by eliminating the obstacles, but by making use of them."[6] These plot twists in life can make us feel like we are being dragged by a rope on a dirt road, jolting over ruts and rocks with no end in sight. Yet somehow we can also believe that there is *more* than this suffering—there is transformation. Do you believe that? Do you believe that this unimaginable adversity could be your path to healing and restoration? Have you discovered more about yourself in hardship or in bliss? Honestly, when I am "in bliss," I am blissfully unaware. Yet there is something about suffering that makes you pause and question yourself. Who am I? Why does this hurt so much? The gift in moving forward after the plot twist is that you get to find the rest of you.

After the sabbatical, I returned to work, but rest, reflection, and repeated honest and hard conversations with those I love most helped me learn how to hold work loosely. Letting go of my need to control every detail of work eased the overwhelming feeling that I had to perform to earn my worth. Jeff and I also decided that when we returned, we would quit every extra activity that we didn't miss while away. This exercise created a freedom to question what we did miss and gracefully shed some excess responsibilities. I slowly learned not to cling to work as my identity because it composed only a part of me. I learned I was so much *more*. I wanted to be content with myself even if I never worked again. I was a listening friend, an adventurous wife, a mother curious to learn more about her daughter, and ultimately a woman who was at peace with herself without any titles to her name. This peace with yourself is for you too, even if you never become the person you imagined yourself to be; you now get the blessed opportunity to become *all* of you.

## LIMITATIONS VERSUS CAPACITY

How do we become *all* we are meant to be? I believe it starts with knowing our limitations and capacity. Knowing your limitations helps you understand your capacity. Capacity is "the maximum amount that something can contain; the amount that something can produce; the ability to do something: a mental, emotional, or physical ability."[7]

If capacity is how much you can hold in this one container called life, then you have to know the limitations of your container. Knowing your limitations helps you know your container size. How much, and what, can I fit into a day? How full can my calendar actually be? You may have the capacity to have six children in your home; I do not. You may have the capacity to join the PTA; I do not. You may have the capacity to work sixty-five hours per week; I do not. Your capacity is not the same as my capacity, but knowing your capacity is key.

Capacity varies by person, so we cannot compare or judge. Yet I often measured others' capacity against my own and decided I didn't measure up. This capacity comparison crept into my thoughts and tore me down. It all started with paying attention to the "shoulds" circling through my brain.

Where did all these "shoulds" come from? We make these judgments on ourselves for not measuring up to some ideal we have construed—the greater capacities of those around us. We must shut down the "shoulds" so we can understand our limitations and capacity.

An easy strategy to help you recognize your capacity is to write down your limitations. Your limitations are beacons guiding you to deeper soul-needs you may be missing in the busyness of life.

Here are a few examples of my limitations:

- Limitation: I can't work all day and then work at night as well.

  Soul need: I need to decompress and relax my brain at night. (I even daydream while at work about curling into bed at night with a book.)
- Limitation: I can't be inside all day.

  Soul need: I need to spend time outside in nature every day. (This can look like going for a walk, working in the garden, or taking my kids to the playground.)
- Limitation: I can't be around people 24/7.

  Soul need: I need alone time when I don't speak to anyone. (If you have small children, you might understand this also includes a no-touching zone.)

Once you have asked yourself all the hard questions and feel like you know your capacity, the next step is establishing safeguards and boundaries to keep it in check. Explore questions like these: How can I protect my calendar from filling up? Do I need to schedule my weekly or daily personal time into my calendar? Maybe I need to talk with my partner about my need to have one hour a day away from the kids and figure out a plan. Maybe I need to limit myself to going out only twice per week. "Your greatest weakness is your strength overplayed," my brother-in-law likes to say, and that couldn't be more evident in the ways I have "pushed through" most moments of my life, with no thought of myself.

Oh, I distinctly remember some of these moments with you. Remember in college when you had surgery and rushed back to campus that same day to play a volleyball game?

**Jeff, it was my last game, and I had to play.**

Yeah, you doped yourself up on painkillers, and I don't think you even remember the game!

**Ha-ha, that's true. But I do remember we won.**

How about when you decided to run a full marathon while working full-time and pushing an eighteen-month-old in the stroller for your entire training?

**I did feel like all I did was work and run for months on end. Why do I keep torturing myself like this?**

Do you see how you had no idea what was too much for yourself? Yet you compare yourself to your triathlete friends when this is the norm for them.

**[Sigh] I can always find someone to compare myself to who seems to be doing it better.**

André, your capacity is not the same as a professional triathlete—someone who does this for their job.

My strength and will to persevere overflowed my capacity and left me weak, empty, and burned-out. No boundaries, no limits, no capacity to give fully to love or work.

## CARE

When our capacity is full, no space is left for self-care. And self-care is critical to loving and living our best life.

In the context of love or work, there is a common myth that productivity supersedes everything else. If we are living a productive life, we are living "the good life." We believe the lies that productivity is more important than rest, productivity is more important than intimacy, productivity is more important than friendships. For us to gain a realization of capacity in our personal lives, we must acknowledge that productivity is not the key to happiness. I had to battle the lie that I needed to do more to be more. I struggled with knowing my limits, and I needed my partner to help me. David Whyte says, "A partner in marriage is a partner in self-revelation."[8] When I shifted from working five days a week to three, the demons I had to battle for keeping my kids in daycare five days a week gnawed at my "lack of productivity" meter and told me I brought less worth to the table. Nevertheless, I persisted.

First day off: I cleaned all day because my hands and head felt like they had to be busy. Also, the guilt factor was at an all-time high. Result: clean house (even the baseboards), capacity still in overload mode.

Second day off: Pruned and cleaned the yard. All day. Children came home to an exhausted, sunburned, dehydrated mom. Result: garden started (sore body), capacity still in overload mode.

Third day off: Jeff kissed me goodbye and said, “André, do something you love today. Do something you never get to do. Do something that makes you happy. *I am giving you permission.*” Those sweet words were like a balm to my aching spirit (and body, because I was still sore from that entire day of gardening). I sat on my couch to ponder his statement. Do something I love. What did I love? I couldn’t remember the last time I asked myself this question.

What do I enjoy doing?

What makes me relax?

What brings me joy?

I had no clue.

I vowed not to move from the couch until I remembered *one* thing I loved to do that was not attached to a “should.” I did love to read. I gazed over at my stack of books next to my bed: business, self-help, spiritual development, and medical literature. All books I *should* read to better myself as a leader, woman, mother, physician assistant, etc. When was the last time I read a book just for fun? Just for pleasure? Decision made, I plopped myself on the couch and purchased the Divergent book series on my Kindle and escaped into the dystopian world of YA fiction. That day I read for hours. I took a nap. I ate ice cream for lunch (because at this point, why not?), and I took a long walk with my dog. It was the *best day ever.*

I had given myself freedom to enjoy an entire day for me. I was filled with energy and love when the kids came home from daycare and felt more like myself than I had in years. My cup was full because my capacity wasn’t. Not everyone can take a full day to themselves, but it can start with a centering moment and self-assessment of the desires of your heart. First, I remind myself that

I am not what I do. Then I perform what I call a "body awareness scan." Here are my questions:

> Where is my mind today? Am I worried, anxious, full of jumbled thoughts? How do I unload that?
> Where is my heart today? Am I hurting, sad, angry, full of joy? What do I do with those feelings?
> Where is my soul today? Do I feel connected to the Divine? Am I at peace? Am I content? How do I honor that?
> Where is my body today? Am I sore? Am I tired? Am I full of pent-up energy? What does that mean my body needs to do?

If I'm worried or anxious, I journal or meditate.

If I'm sad or angry, I take time to go for a walk and process my emotions before I engage with others.

If I'm sore, I stretch or do yoga.

You can do this too. Sometimes you need someone to give you permission, like Jeff gave me. So here it is: I give you permission to scan your body and give yourself what you need. Even if you have only an hour while the kids are napping, instead of cleaning up like you always do, take a quick body assessment and take a nap if that's what your body needs. Maybe you have only an hour on your lunch break. Do a body assessment before your lunch break and determine if you need to take a walk during lunch or get away to a quiet place for a moment. We all can take a minute to listen to ourselves. If this book is nothing else, please let it be your permission slip to take a nap, get your nails done, eat some chocolate, order takeout, and most importantly, let go of your "shoulds."

Here are some great questions to get you started on learning your needs and desires to sustain health in love and work:[9]

- What invigorates my life? (What brings me joy?)
- What sustains my soul? (What brings me peace?)
- What do I need to let go of? (What "shoulds" do I need to release?)
- What do I need to hold on to? (What is healthy that I need to keep?)

Here is a visual example that might help you process through the questions. You can fill in the quadrants with words or pictures that come to mind.[10]

The next step is very important: share your needs with your partner. Jeff now understands my three basic soul needs. And the best part is that he helps me keep them a priority. Through discussion, we identified healthy actions based on my limitations and soul needs.

Maintaining love and work is possible only if you and your partner are healthy, and being healthy means knowing your capacity and caring for yourself. Research tells us we are a society of working men and women, moms and dads, raising children, trying our best, but in doing so we've blown the lids off our personal capacity meters—leaving many of us exhausted, overwhelmed, and guilt-ridden. Yet we've discovered there are strategies, both individually and as couples, to help us keep our capacities in check. Through recognizing our own breaking points, engaging in vulnerable discussion, being willing to give each other permission slips, and identifying space for care, we grow stronger. Today you received a special permission slip that gives you the freedom to look inward, think about what you love, and stand in that space—for a minute, a day, three months. Know that every second you pour on care for you, you're creating more capacity for love and work to bloom. Everyone grows and blooms differently, but our personal favorite way is to get away. And we wouldn't be truly *us* if we didn't have a good fight first. (Sigh. Just keep reading.)

## TALK ABOUT IT

Before you move forward, take a moment to answer these questions on your own and invite your partner to discuss them with you.

1. When was a time you felt burnout or exhaustion? How did others help you or hurt you in that season?
2. Do you have a strength you're overplaying right now? What capacity checks do you need to employ to contain it?
3. Has the tension between rest and productivity ever been a challenge for you? How do you best overcome that tension?

4. What is one thing you could do for yourself to minimize exhaustion? How can you apply it in your life?

## DO A CHALLENGE

We all need creative ideas for taking what we read and putting it into practice. Share your experience with others and tag @loveorwork #loveorwork.

***Care for yourself.*** Ask your partner for a day to yourself. Go and do something that reinvigorates your life. No "shoulds." No work. No honey-do list. No parenting. No phone. No shame. Take some time to process the four questions that André asked in this chapter. When you get home, encourage your partner to take a day next.

## LISTEN UP

Add to this journey by listening to a free podcast that relates to this chapter and will give you even more to process. Go to www.loveorwork.com/listenup.

### Opposites Attract: Aaron and Shauna Niequist (Episode 52)

Listen to Aaron and Shauna share how they changed the definition of a "successful" day to be more about connection than the accomplishment of tasks. Aaron is a musician and author of the book *The Eternal Current*, and Shauna is the *New York Times* bestselling author of *Present Over Perfect*.

WHENEVER WE GO AWAY, it BRINGS US CLOSER TOGETHER.

-JEFF SHinABARGER-

#LOVE or WORK

CHAPTER 8

# *Get Away*

## JEFF

**Happiness consists of living each day as if it were the first day of your honeymoon and the last day of your vacation.**

—LEO TOLSTOY

Taking time off from work rarely starts out with relaxation; it usually begins with dirty laundry. For some reason the progression of heading out on vacation always seems to lead to disagreements on multiple fronts.

I'm usually the instigator. It's the night before we take off on a trip, and I load the washer. The process begins with collecting all the clothes hampers and building a huge laundry mountain in front of the washer. Turning on that first load is like winning a raucous game of King of the Mountain.

**And since your investment peaked at round one, hoping you'll transfer clothes from the washer to the dryer is completely futile.**

Yes. Starting things is a gift I freely give to our family.

**But finishing is the growth edge the rest of us in the world need you to work on.**

This is exactly what I'm trying to explain. It starts with laundry. Then it quickly moves to a debate about whether we can share a suitcase or whether we each should have our own luggage.

**Then it's a battle about what time we really need to leave in the morning.**

No later than 7:00 a.m. We have to beat traffic.

**I'll be getting up at 6:45, and we'll see what time we hit the road.**

Or if we're flying, we need to arrive two hours ahead of time.

**Or forty-five minutes before takeoff.**

No. Remember that time you missed the plane coming back from New York?

**Right. See, we all have opportunities to grow.**

Like you always needing a spotless house before we leave on vacation. What's the deal with that?

**There's nothing better than coming home to a clean house. And what about your obsession with showering before we can get on the road?**

Showers are a necessity. When we finally get loaded up and start on our way, it's usually followed by a solid hour of unleashing every frustration that has been building over the last month.

**Yup, every time. Sometimes in the car and other times at the gate of our plane.**

We are so focused on just trying to make it to the vacation that we neglect each other in the preparation.

**And we both apologize because we know we've just needed time with each other. And then we make up and start having fun.**

And I find you some Junior Mints.

**While also buying yourself some gummy bears.**

"Isn't it amazing how much stuff we get done the day before vacation?" The great motivational speaker Zig Ziglar was exactly right—we work so hard to get away that we often neglect the people with whom we are trying to escape. It might take time to reconnect, but it's worth it.

Once we get on the road, we proceed to release the busyness of the past few weeks, remembering what we love about each other and gaining a fresh perspective. After working so hard to be on vacation, we need time to shift into relaxation mode. It's not uncommon to be a few days into our vacation before we get a really good night's sleep.

Going away always brings us closer together. When our family is in a new place, we create new memories. The time off encourages us to release stressors and make space for love to flow in. But getting to that place of rest and rejuvenation seems really hard. Is that why more of us don't get away? Is it the process of getting away that keeps us from going? Once we get there, we understand how shared experiences enhance family connection. What keeps us from these shared experiences?

One of our most surprising research findings was related to the use (or disuse) of vacation time. For working couples trying to sustain work and love, you'd think that taking vacation time would be a priority. Rest and relaxation. White-sand beaches and popsicle stands. Board games and spike ball. Books and massages. But these vacation must-haves aren't a reality.

Our findings show that the majority of people we surveyed do *not* use paid vacation leave. Specifically, 59 percent do not use all the annual vacation days their workplace offers. Let that sink in: nearly six out of ten people do not use their paid vacation days! If you stood ten people in line at your work and told them all to go on vacation and you would pay them to leave, only four of them would go. In addition, only one-quarter of the people interviewed take one "getaway" trip per year. In 2018, Americans left more than 768 million vacations days unused in the workforce.[1] That may give us a clue as to why we all feel exhausted.

Are you one of those people who doesn't use paid days off? Isn't vacation time intended to be taken and used? When did we begin passing up getaways with family and friends in favor of work? Is it possible that productivity in the workforce is tipping the scales away from popsicles with the family?

It's not surprising that productivity and achievement are top values in the United States. But the emphasis we put on those two ideals places work over family time—and vacation time. The US is the only developed country in the world without a single legally required paid vacation day or holiday. By law, every country in the European Union requires at least four workweeks of paid vacation.[2] One-fourth of the workforce in America is not granted any vacation. The American dream has created a culture where productivity supersedes rest. In our research, about 4 percent of respondents who didn't take vacation said it was because they don't receive vacation days. Those who aren't given vacation *can't* take it, and for participants in our study, many who are given vacation *don't* take it. This is not the American dream. This is a nightmare.

Our findings indicate that the majority of the people reading this book have a job that tells them to take time off and they don't. I've struggled with taking time off myself. We all have great intentions and ambitious fantasies of places to go and people to see, but too often our work holds us back. When work productivity replaces family possibilities, it's time for a new perspective.

I understand the pressures that exist in always wanting to be a contributor in my work and the struggle of releasing the responsibility. Learning from a young age to follow my dad's advice as a nineteen-year-old eager-to-please intern has made it difficult to accept taking time off. "Jeff, be the first person into work and the last person to leave. Then you will get more opportunities. If they give you something to do, get it done that day. Then the next day they will entrust you with something even more important." His pep talk has guided my approach to my work ever since. That summer I did everything asked of me (and more), and because of that, I was given more and more to do. This mindset and the accompanying habits became my work ethic, but it also set me up for an unsustainable lifestyle when I got married and started having kids. I appreciate the advice my dad gave, but I took it to an unhealthy, workaholic level.

This advice became hard to shake. As a leader of an organization, I thought I needed to be present for everything. If there was a meeting, I needed to be in it. If there was an event, I needed to be at it. I needed to be the guy opening the doors. This mentality helped me grow my influence, but it started an unhealthy pattern. It also created an untenable work environment for others. Worst of all, it created an unsustainable family life. I had created a culture where everyone needed to be at everything. Everyone needed to come early. Everyone needed to stay late. Work was everything. The mission had become work > love.

My approach to work needed to change, and for that to happen, *I* needed to change. It would take some serious intentionality on my part to integrate a new way of living into an old way of doing. But I know now that one of the most liberating things about change is pouring into the things you love, taking a step away from the repetition of work and leaning in to those you love.

## WHY DON'T WE TAKE VACATIONS?

I needed to change my own work > vacation scenario. Workdays had become the hardest days. Too many meetings. A disagreement with a client (or maybe three), and not enough time to get to what I needed to complete. Then I'd rush home from work exhausted. Make dinner. War with the kids to get them to eat something green on their plate. Clean up the kitchen. Play with the children and remember why I love them again. Tackle the bedtime rituals—wrestle the kids into pajamas, brush teeth, put them to bed. Then lie on the couch, check email, social media, see a friend living his best life on a beach more perfect than any you have ever experienced. And finally, go to bed.

The reality is that I'm exhausted because the pressure to produce and succeed at work is compounded by daily battles over green-bean consumption and cavity-free teeth at home. I need a break to catch up on sleep, have a drink by the pool, and reserve enough energy for a night with my spouse. That friend on social media doesn't help, because now I also need to find time to work out in order to put on that swimsuit. This is the vortex, and only after I've scored a perfect ten in all categories can I even think about planning a vacation, packing four people's stuff, and enduring the whining about when we're going to get there. Not to mention scheduling ahead to cover the extra work that piles up while I'm away.

And just like that, before the opening music is done, the dream has died.

Fifty-nine percent of us aren't refusing to take a vacation because we don't want one. We all want to go away; we just don't know how to make this luxury a reality. This is my story. My family's story matches our findings; we wanted an adventurous story, but we didn't know where to begin. Why? Why can't we just pack up and use the time we're supposed to be taking?

So we asked: "Why are your vacation days untaken?" The most common reason adults do not use all their paid time off is because they are saving them—generally or specifically for emergencies or sickness (13 percent). Additionally, they have too much work or too many work responsibilities (11 percent) or simply are too busy (7 percent).

Saving time off for emergencies is understandable, responsible. But if we keep thinking this way forever, the real emergency will be your marriage, and all the time you saved (and more) will be spent on trying to fix your relationship. The truth is that most people don't regret stepping out of the hustle and bustle of work and taking a vacation. But we know many people who have regretted not taking the extra (and allowed) time with the people they love.

However, 11 percent of our respondents said they just don't use the days given to them. So they let time go by, life happens, and oops, maybe next year. That's just sad. It's not that hard to make a plan and get away. We'll talk about how to do it below.

To the 11 percent who said they feel unable to take time off because of too much work or too many work responsibilities: *I get it.* But this feeling is an illusion. It implies you think you're too important to miss work or the work is too important to miss you. And whether true or not, this mindset leads to an unsustainable way of living and an inflated sense of self-importance. Find help, delegate, set boundaries, and get some perspective. Later we'll discuss some ways we can allow our coworkers to rise up so we can finally rest up.

Nine percent of our respondents said they can't afford to travel. We hear this too. But getting away doesn't mean you have to spend a ton of money or even leave your house. The point is to *get away* from work. Sometimes staycations work just as well. You don't have to travel to spend quality time with your family. The goal is to separate from work and build stronger connections among family members.

The responsibilities of life can feel like a knotted ball of Christmas lights we pull out of the box the first day of December: intertwined so thoroughly that unwinding them can seem impossible. We are stuck. We can't separate from the urgent requests because of the constant access to work through our phone in-hand. We can't loosen the calendar because of commitments. We can't see beyond the task list because it guides the ins and outs of every day. Instead of trying to find one knot to untangle, we choose to set aside the whole ball of responsibilities, go to sleep, and think about it another day.

Sometimes we must decide to step away from our work to remind ourselves of the purpose we are trying to live. Without dedicated moments when we can slow down productivity, remember our sense of calling, and take time for our first love, we will forget why we are doing what we are made to do. Getting away will either reinvigorate our mission or send us in a different direction. Both can be good, but if we want it to happen, getting away is a must.

## WHAT IF YOU WENT AWAY MORE?

We love to travel, explore, and see new things. Finding a new coffee shop. Taking a walk in a new city. Going for a bike ride. It energizes us. My imagination always expands when I see creative expressions in uncomfortable places by unpredictable people. To keep things interesting, we need to see interesting new things. We need to do interesting new things. We need to be in interesting new places. There's not much to talk about when life is not new and different. Even risky, scary new things are shared experiences that force us closer. These shared experiences give us plenty to talk about and always strengthen our connection with one another.

As a family, we commit to travel out of the country every year to introduce our children to different cultures. We started this practice before the kids turned two. And let's just acknowledge that traveling with kids under four can be more work than relaxation. But we are teaching our kids to see the world. And accepting and adapting to different cultures is easier for kids than adults. When kids meet people from different cultures, they don't question the differences as much.

Now, we have a bit of an extreme view on time off for the average household, but we believe it's part of what refreshes our commitment to love and work. We take one month off every year, which is much more common in Europe than in America. But when you see what an extended period away will do for you and your family, for your love, and for your work, you'll be hooked.

How do you make this happen? Enter Nikolle and José Reyes, cofounders of the Metaleap Creative design firm.[3] I remember the first time we heard about them taking a month off in the summer with their two children. Our ears instantly perked up. We watched their journey on their family travel blog as they rented a VW and drove across England one summer. Seeing them a couple of months later, we drilled them with questions. What about the kids' activities? What about all the people on your team? Did you miss a bunch of things? Did your absence negatively impact your business?

They answered all our questions, and our dream became more of a reality. To be able to take a month off each year, they had to do some major planning—it actually took ten years of dreaming and waiting to get to it. They saved their money. Their team took responsibility. They communicated with their clients what was happening, and all of them wished they were doing the same thing. Maybe most surprisingly, their planned time off created deeper relationships with their clients and team. They planned their time off in the summer so it didn't interfere with the kids' school. Their family grew extra close, and after one year, they wanted to go away every year. José puts up an away message that says, "I'm out with my family. I will not get your message. Email me back after this date." And then he turns on auto-delete. You read that right: *auto-delete*!

Another nugget of wisdom they graciously shared with us was the gift of going to "no-place-to-be" and handing some decision-making over to their kids. When we're in a place with no agenda and no specific place to be, we can do anything. There is no place to "be." Through this yearly experience and the opportunity to take part in the planning, the kids have developed leadership and character-building skills. To boot, some of the choices the kids made were ones the parents never would have chosen, and they led to even better shared adventures and uncommon experiences. When Nikolle and José told us about their annual liberating escape, (a) I thought it was crazy, and (b) I had to try it.

So it was done. One month. Every year. And we have found

this goodness to be true. Our kids' decisions have taken us off the beaten path and wound us through bubble gum alley (where subsequently everyone sticks their gum). While someplace between highly unsanitary and glorious, we ditched the road map and explored. We rode horses to see howler monkeys. We found a beach that sparkled like gold. We all jumped off a tall pier into the ocean because the courage of the kids inspired us to do it. Our kids led the charge on no-place-to-be vacations. We empowered them to chart the course and pilot the ship and created a space to listen to their adventures. And choosing the road less traveled has, in epic form, made all the difference. Dare to disrupt normal life. Learn about a world that might be confusing, uncomfortable, and a bit dangerous, and let it lead you to a far better life than you have yet experienced.

*To create kids who will change the world, it is important for them to see the world.*

We adults get stuck in a rut and tell ourselves we can't take vacation days and engage our children in seeing the world. We take our kids to school. We go to work. We separate. We divide. We try to conquer individually. André has a girls' night. I get a guys' night. Jada goes to dance. Neko goes to golf. André works out. I go to the dog park. Vacation seemed like an impossible dream. But we put our foot down.

Taking a month off of work is not a magical solution, and it's not even possible for everyone. Your work may not allow for this kind of time away. I get that. But can you take *more* time away than you are currently taking? For you it might mean progressing toward separating more from work. Consider also what both you and your partner want and need. Our personalities caused us to make a shocking shift. Yours and your reality are different. If you are one of the 59 percent who don't use vacation days, maybe your first goal should be to *do just that*. Use the time you have to fight the exhaustion. What could it look like for you? How could you do it?

## MAKE AN ANNUAL PLAN

How you get away might look completely different from the way we do it, but for the love of all things love and work, *do it*. Taking time off won't just happen; you have to prepare for it. We knew we wanted to get away, but we needed to figure out how to do it. We stepped back and thought about what the year ahead would look like. We created an annual calendar and a shared calendar. We took control away from work and zeroed in on our vacation time. We prioritized a plan.

Only 25 percent of couples in our research make a plan or vision for their year, and only 31 percent share a calendar. A shared calendar streamlines your life and gets you on the same page with your partner. It says, "We planned this time off together. We value this time to explore." To the vast majority of couples who wonder how to better fill their evenings, to change what needs to be changed, or to plan for the future: Sit. Talk. Share a calendar. Dream. Plan your time off together. Look ahead and see the slow times. See the busy times. See what your family could do together in the coming year.

Try to take off a month every year, or chart your own course. But create a *shared plan* for your year. Here's how we look at our year.

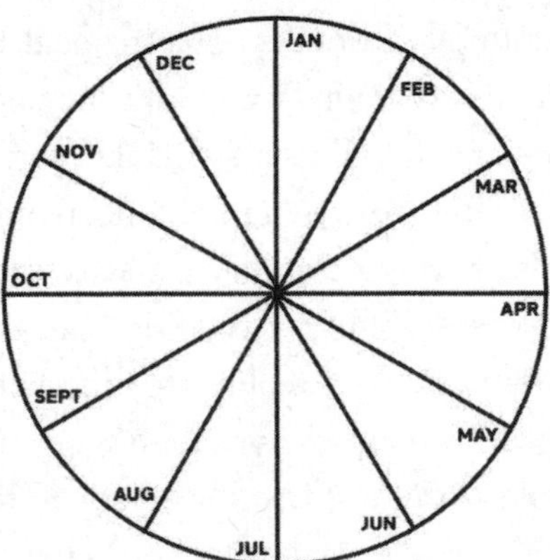

We highlight the "busy time" slices, because we know they exist. If you work in retail and try to take a vacation in November or December, that won't be ideal. That's the busy season, so shade those months off. Know your busy season.

For me, the busy season is July and early August, and I speak in February, March, September, and October. So we shade out those times. We do the same with André's schedule and our kids' schedules, working around their school calendar and activities.

Notice any overlapping portions on the pie graph; these are *really busy* seasons. Any open slices are the spaces to claim for family time. For us, it's June. We live for it all year. We would not make it without June.

I know this can seem impossible. Many people tell us they can't afford to do this kind of thing. But we couldn't afford *not* to take time off and be with one another. The way we plan isn't *the* solution; it has been *our* solution. Find yours.

The big takeaway is that if you want to make time away a reality for your family, you will need to intentionally claim those days of the year and then plan to make it happen—it never just happens on its own.

Once you identify and claim the time, then you can start to share the plan with others.

The next phase is simple but important. Start a digital calendar and share it with your partner. Block off the dates you agree to, and *voilà*. Time claimed. We've found the most resourceful time to do this planning as a couple is the week between Christmas and New Year's. André and I have a planning session over a cup of coffee with minimal distractions. We bring computers. We bring ideas. It's a special, serious date focused on claiming family time and getting away, ensuring we don't simply keep working and miss out.

Some key questions we explore:

- What do we need individually to sustain work, a happy marriage, and our family?
- What do we need as a couple to grow together?
- What do we need to work on with our kids?
- How can we help each other make our dreams for work a reality?
- How will we get away this year?

## CREATING A VACATION CULTURE

The more we openly communicate and prioritize this way of "claiming" time together, the more we established a culture of partnership and togetherness within our family. As I mentioned earlier, my workaholic tendencies started as a nineteen-year-old intern and eventually created an unhealthy culture in my work and family. As I changed, our organizational culture changed. It only takes one person to set a new standard. Now vacations are openly encouraged, celebrated, and shared. For birthdays we often give teammates gift cards for Airbnb or Delta SkyMiles to make it easier for them to get away. Taking time off gives all of us extra energy, fresh perspective, and a renewed focus on goals. It also directly addresses the dissatisfaction we experience in life and affords a greater appreciation for different cultures and the world. After a busy season comes a strategic rest season. Pinpoint the busy season, and attach the rest season at its heels.

During that season of rest, on your well-deserved getaway (and at the end of each workday), one of the best things you can do happens behind closed eyes. Almost half of our respondents want more sleep. *Claim it.* Claim it on vacation. Claim it at the end of the day. Plan it if you have to, but do it because you must. Vacation is a perfect time to reset internal clocks and redefine REM cycles. Additional areas of dissatisfaction in our research were too little time to exercise, too little time with family, too little intimacy and time spent with one's partner, too few adventures in life, and (shocker) too much stress at work. All these feelings are understandable, valid, and reverberate through the greater American culture. And (drumroll, please) *all* can be addressed and solved by getting away.

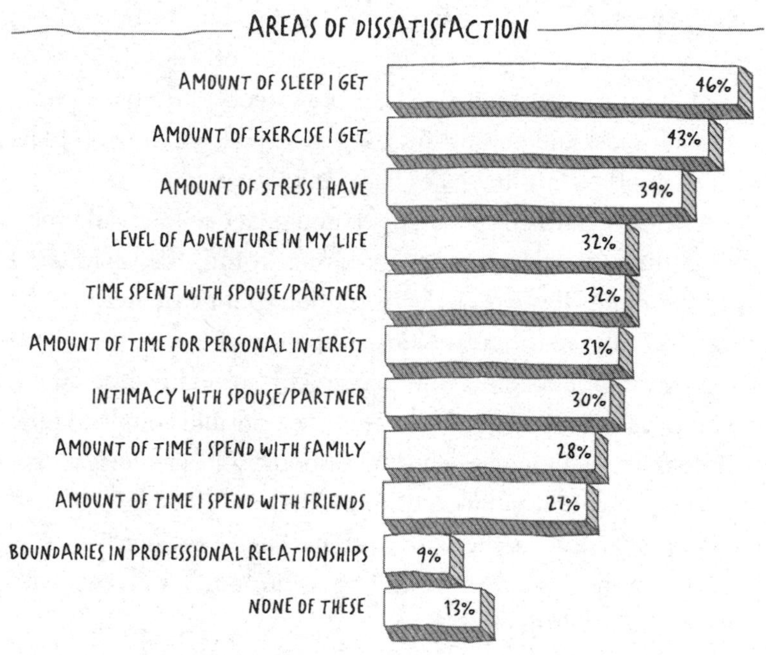


## THE BENEFITS OF GETTING AWAY

Getting away directly addresses our greatest dissatisfaction in life and gives us a glimpse of better days. Slowing down and separating from work creates a healthier version of ourselves.

Getting away is good for our health. The 1992 Framingham Heart Study, which still stands as the gold standard for long-term health studies, tracked workers over twenty years. It found that "men who don't take vacations were 30% more likely to have a heart attack and for women it went up to 50%."[4] Getting away plays a role in reducing stress, preventing heart disease, improving sleep, and enhancing productivity. It also increases awe and whimsy and creates an opportunity for adventure.[5]

Moreover, getting away creates a healthier family. Our family explores, learns, and grows closer together. Our relationships with one another strengthen. We share uncommon experiences, make new memories, and laugh more freely. For André and me, getting away invites more flirting with each other and increases sexual interest in each other. These are direct results of claiming a season of rest and getting away together. Taking time off to be with each other tips the scales back in love's favor.

A healthy team culture that encourages, celebrates, and actually requires vacation time helps love win too. Kayla, whom I call "the glue," has worked with me for about three years. She works full-time and has two kids under the age of two, and she keeps everything together and ticking at Plywood People. She is a planner, a doer, and one of the most responsible people I know. She doesn't get a ton of sleep. The responsibility she feels creeps into every moment of her day, and sometimes it weighs on her. Everywhere she goes she serves others—her kids, her husband, her friends, and often André and me. She handles all of it with class and commitment.

Last fall Kayla's husband, Joseph, reached out to me about wanting to surprise her and take her away on a trip to Tulum, Mexico—a dream of hers. She needed it. They needed it. And as a team, we were thrilled to be a part of making her dream happen. We also realized we needed to be set up to fully operate with her away.

Over dinner, the night before they left, Kayla learned the bags were packed and they were leaving first thing in the morning and the kids were getting their own vacation with their grandparents. One of my favorite messages I received that year was from Kayla: "So I'm going to Mexico tomorrow morning, but it sounds like you already know that." When Kayla came back, she was rested and reported feeling more productive and energized than before. The time away made her a better wife, mom, and teammate.

It's not enough to get away; it's also our responsibility to foster a work culture of getting away for those with whom we work. Help other people make getting away possible. In an era when finding good talent is a constant tension, a work culture that actively encourages people to take a vacation is one that potential employees will want to join. Getting away breeds creativity for those away while simultaneously creating space for people in the office to lead in ways they don't normally get to. Taking time off requires shared responsibility, opens doors to new ways of thinking, and invites all of us to be better.

## HOW TO AFFORD IT

We've created a road map for dreaming, claiming our time, and fostering a work culture that values time away. The next step is to get out of town (or at least out of the office) without breaking the bank. Here are four quick tips to make this possible:

- Save up.
- Use miles.
- Ask for more time.
- Ask for the "good guy" discount.

**Really? You're going to give four tips for taking vacations?**

Yes, everyone asks us for these. And the good guy discount is the secret sauce.

**It is literally the most embarrassing thing ever.**

Has it literally saved us thousands of dollars?

**It has saved us thousands of dollars. So go ahead.**

Ask for the good guy (or good girl) discount. We prioritize our places we travel by where we get the best deal. And all because we (when I say we, I mean me) ask for the "good guy" deal. It's a real thing. You might be asking, what is a good guy deal? Well, I'm a good guy, so I ask if they have discounts for good people.

**It's ridiculous. But it works, literally every time. Call the hotel and ask. Message the house owner and ask. We prioritize our places based on who says yes to the proposed good deal (which Jeff made up).**

Remember that one time I asked for a good guy discount at the Nike store?

**I can't believe they gave it to you.**

I got a 20 percent discount. I first heard about this strategy on This American Life.[6] It's brilliant.

**It's . . . something. I will never do it, but I appreciate your asks.**

Save your money and your miles. What you invest money and time in will show what you love.

**It takes a year of saving for us to go away. We have to put away money every month of the year for the one month we go away.**

We have never regretted spending money on family adventures, ever.

**That is very true.**

**It's hard to get raises, but getting more time off is easier. Instead of asking for more money, ask for more time.**

Exactly. Negotiate your time, not just your paycheck.

We save up time, money, and air miles, and that's how we afford to take time off.

Let's revisit our dreadful VW van experience. From a photographer's perspective, it yielded some amazing photos, but from a relaxation perspective, it was hard because we were always on the move from campground to beach town, and it was tough to get a good night's sleep on a two-inch-pad bed. The living quarters were small, and we all had to take turns sleeping with Neko because he sleeps like a squirrelly squirrel.

But I will never forget what happened when we got home. The kids headed to their rooms to sleep in their beds while André and I went to our master bedroom and cozied into our king bed. We had all the room in the world. The next morning, the kids came running down the hall and jumped into each side of the bed and snuggled in. We could tell something wasn't quite right. "What's wrong?" we asked the kids. Neko answered for the two of them: "We like being home, but it feels like you are so far away! We wanted to be closer to you." André and I looked at each other, and our hearts swelled. We each hugged them, and there, in the gigantic bed, we found our reason for that vacation. Not to mention a great love.

Such moments don't just happen. That difficult trip physically and emotionally brought us closer together. Every time we go away, it happens. It's rarely the perfectly planned things that bring us together. It is the unplanned moments that couldn't have happened unless we chose to get away. So save up, use your miles, ask for more time, and ask for the discount.

Now that you've made a plan to get away, it's time to talk about what you'll be doing with that free time. Time for the sex talk. Keep reading to find the chapter you've been waiting for—or potentially the one you already jumped ahead to and read first.

## TALK ABOUT IT

Before you move forward, take a moment to answer these questions on your own and invite your partner to discuss them with you.

1. How do your trips normally begin? Take a moment to walk through the play-by-play and laugh about how predictable we all are.
2. Are you and your family taking full advantage of vacations? How is that impacting the closeness of your relationships?
3. How does your work culture positively or negatively impact your view of vacation? How can you help create a better culture?
4. When are the busy times on each of your calendars? How can you make an annual plan to commit to getting away?

## DO A CHALLENGE

We all need creative ideas for taking what we read and putting it into practice. Share your experience with others and tag @loveorwork #loveorwork.

***Plan a one-night stand.*** That's right. A one-night stand with your *every* night partner. Pick a place. Make a plan. Put it on the calendar. Commit to one night. Make it happen (in more ways than one). You'll be surprised how getting away will make you want to use your vacation days even more.

## LISTEN UP

Add to this journey by listening to a free podcast that relates to this chapter and will give you even more to process. Go to www.loveorwork.com/listenup.

**Working Together, Side by Side: Nikolle and José Reyes (Episode 38)**

To hear more about how another family packs up and leaves every year, listen to Nikolle and José Reyes talk about the practical ways they make it happen! José and Nikolle are the founders of Metaleap Creative, an Atlanta-based agency working with brands from Coca-Cola to *In Touch* magazine.

DESPITE OUR SEXUAL HISTORY, WE CAN FIND FREEDOM IN OUR SEXUAL HEALTH TODAY.

—André Shinabarger and Jeff Shinabarger—

#LOVE or WORK

CHAPTER 9

# *Sex Talk*

## JEFF AND ANDRÉ

**Marriage is not the end of romance, it is the beginning.**

—ESTHER PEREL

**I can't believe we are writing a chapter on sex. Just writing that word on a page is making me break out in a sweat.**

I mean, it's the one chapter every person will read. Let's be honest: if I bought this book, I would jump ahead and read this chapter first.

**Of course you would, Jeff, but seriously, this is scary!**

Sex is the number one thing everyone needs to talk about and wants to talk about, yet no one is talking about it.

**I get that, yet it also feels like it should stay private.**

True. I hope that readers don't just minimize our stories,

but that our openness will cause couples to be more open themselves. The truth is that it will be very difficult for couples to stay in love without talking about sex.

**And let's not forget that we have parents and children who could read this!**

**MOM AND DAD! STOP RIGHT HERE. FOR THE LOVE OF ALL THAT IS HOLY, MOVE TO THE NEXT CHAPTER. NOTHING FOR YOU HERE.**

The real question is, will you have our kids read this one day?

**Wow. It's getting real.**

Let's go ahead and begin with the elephant in the room: Sex is complicated!

It can cause hurt and joy.

It can be extremely vulnerable and also guarded.

It can be emotional or just practical.

It can uplift or tear down.

It can bring pleasure or pain.

It can be no big deal or a very big deal.

It can have good seasons and bad.

It can bring unity or division.

It can be many things at once.

How can one act be all these things at the same time? How does it transcend every parameter we put around it? Every time we label it or seem to grasp one aspect of it, we find a new layer of complexity or awesomeness. Our ideas about sex are influenced by so many opposing factors, such as family history, cultural expectations, movies, past experiences, and porn. And this isn't even the tip of the iceberg when you consider different variances of sexuality or even the spectrum of sexuality that exists.

First, let's strip things down (grin): we are not sex therapists or experts. We are two heterosexual humans in a monogamous relationship. This means we do not understand all the variances of sexuality. Our experiences are limited, but we do believe in the importance of positive sexual health and have seen how it has positively impacted our story personally, relationally, and even professionally. So if our journey can be helpful or freeing, well, here goes nothing (deep breath in, deep breath out).

Our intent in this chapter is to (1) invite healing freedom into your relationship, (2) promote conversation about sex between you and your partner, and (3) share how sex can improve both love and work, making them that much sweeter. You won't hear that one way is the only way, because we don't believe it. You won't hear any shaming or judgment, because every moment in your story matters, even the most difficult and painful ones. You won't hear us tell you to "get it together," because we are all messes trying to figure out this confusing and vulnerable relational element together. So let's talk about the thing that everyone wants to talk about, but no one seems to talk about.

Let's talk about sex, baby.

## START WITH YOUR PAST

I (André) was raised in a very conservative evangelical family, yet my mom was a nurse. So while my life felt sheltered from "bad words," she taught me all the correct terminology from a young age. No one had a "wee-wee" or "privates"; you had a penis or vulva/vagina. Everything was clinical. When I became a premed major, everything I learned about sex was "Penis inserts into vagina, sperm meets egg, and unless using protection, baby will be made and/or STDs will be contracted." Very practical. I was a big rule follower, so if you told me that sex = STDs, well then, get that penis as far away from me as possible.

It's no shocker I naturally fell into the abstinence camp and eventually, in the 1990s, into the Purity Movement. Some of you are like, "What?" Yes, it was a real thing. The Purity Movement was big with white evangelicals, and many teenagers took a pledge to remain sexually abstinent until their wedding day. This coexisted with a firm warning, often unstated but palpably felt: sex was wrong and would lead to horrible consequences.

I was all in. I was a straight-A, straitlaced young woman who fell into the perfect box that this movement placed around me. I packaged my sexuality into a tightly sealed impenetrable box (yes, I've heard this euphemism) and I shipped that box to the land of Far-far-away, never to be seen or discussed again. Please note that I understand that I fall into the minority with this decision of abstinence until marriage. In our society today, this choice is unusual, and more commonly the majority of you readers have had multiple sexual experiences before committing to a long-term partnership. Studies show that by age twenty, 75 percent of Americans have had premarital sex, and that statistic increases to 95 percent by age forty-four.[1]

I get it, I'm a lone wolf in this category, but don't let my unusual beginning deter you from the *rest of the story*.

Then we got married. And everything was supposed to change. Sex wasn't wrong anymore. It was supposed to be very right. It just wasn't that easy.

**How can something be bad your entire life, then in one thirty-minute wedding ceremony it's suddenly good?**

This reminds me of our debate when we first got married. You were dead set on not getting a clear shower curtain.

**Well, I didn't want you all up in my business while I was cleaning myself!**

I was like, that's the point! I liked the visual of

you in the shower. You had so many negative thoughts about your body and the freedom of sharing our bodies with each other.

**Yes, that was definitely how sexually unliberated I was at that time.**

I had to find ways to break down that box of yours. Let's be honest: you didn't even realize that this was going to be the beginning of us being naked all the time together.

**I was so clueless. How in the world did you stick with me all that time?**

It was definitely confusing and it wasn't something that changed quickly. Neither of us fully understood what was going on. I'm a dude with a beautiful wife! In my mind, we were going to be having sex for a long time and we'd figure it out.

So how in the world did I ever open that box, you ask? Well, we had sex. And it was so disappointing. I followed the moral code perfectly, and then it turned out to be such a letdown. Why did the perfect Christian formula A + B not = C? All these ideas of what I thought sex should be: romantic, intimate, cosmic—and instead it was just . . . not. The first time I felt weird and insecure, my brain wouldn't shut down (*Am I doing this right?*), and then it was over.

So I did what any modern woman would do: I turned to Google to ensure this was normal. Lo and behold, *it was*! Google affirmed that I was not the only person in my own head and unable to achieve an orgasm the first time.[2] I chalked it up to my inexperience and figured practice would make perfect. Because if there was one thing I was good at during that time, it was working to perfection.

What I failed to realize was there was one itty-bitty flaw

(okay, monstrous holes) in my thinking. I never thought about how sending my box to the land of Far-far-away would affect me later. Essentially, I boxed up my sexuality as if it were not a part of my created being and sent it packing. The freedom to own or explore my sexuality was foreign to me. I'd blocked off a whole portion of who I was for years, out of fear and striving for my idea of perfection, but mostly out of trying to please God (and what I was told God wanted). Little did I know how much damage this would cause me years down the line, when in the blink of a wedding, I was suddenly permitted, nay, expected to enjoy sex. How in the world are people supposed to integrate this core part of themselves and share it within marriage after shipping it away many moons ago? I had separated myself from my sexuality for so long, I didn't have a clue how to get it back. In my head, sexuality was in the "bad" category, and then suddenly it was supposed to be good.

Meanwhile, most men were educated through porn long before their first experience. I saw my first *Playboy* magazine in fifth grade in the closet of the assistant pastor of our church. From that day forward my view of sex was forever tainted. My initial expectations were completely unrealistic. And this was a big problem for us. My unrealistic expectations and your body dissociation set us up for a disastrous beginning.

**That reminds me of one of my favorite quotes from actress and activist Jameela Jamil: "Learning sex from pornography is like learning to drive from *The Fast and the Furious*. A terrible idea."**

My story was different from your story. We all enter the sexual relationship we have with our partner with different expectations, different past experiences, and different examples of what sex could or even should be. So to say we were off to a rough start is an understatement.

**I was disconnected from my body and my sexuality, and you had unrealistic sexual expectations that were rooted in selfish desires.**

It's true. I was going into sex with the mentality of what you could do for me. It was unequal and unfair, and I didn't fully realize it until about eight years into our marriage. And even though I was technically getting what I wanted, it wasn't really connecting with what you needed. This disconnect caused me to feel both sad and confused.

I'm sure you have your own experiences. Maybe a dominant person made you feel small. Maybe you developed early and became the brunt of objectification or unwelcome attention by adults. Maybe you were emotionally or sexually abused. Maybe you were confused about your attractions and unsure about your identity. There are so many ways we are made to feel ashamed of our sexuality and our bodies. Yet the truth is that we all have an inherent dignity and worth that is a pure gift from our divine Creator.

It has taken me a long time to understand that we are spiritual, sexual, emotional, physical beings whom God called good from the very beginning. The first descriptor of us from the Creator was that we were good. We didn't have to earn one thing from God. Our dignity was given to us freely and unconditionally from the very beginning, and God wants us to live in that wholeness. God made us sexual and wants us to feel free and loved in our sexuality. And this sexual health is a right for *all*, not just certain people. Everybody, every *body* is invited to the party of experiencing their full sexual selves.

Before I share about how I found my own sexual health, let's define the phrase. The World Health Organization defines sexual health this way:

> a state of physical, emotional, mental and social well-being in relation to sexuality; not merely the absence of disease, dysfunction or infirmity. Sexual health requires a positive and respectful approach to sexuality and sexual relationships, as well as the possibility of having pleasurable and safe sexual experiences, free of coercion, discrimination and violence. For sexual health to be attained and maintained, the sexual rights of all persons must be respected, protected and fulfilled.[3]

When we acknowledge our disturbing or deficient sexual education and unique sexual pasts, we can recognize how these have tainted our current sexual health and open our minds to a new way. After years of consistent difficulties and challenges with sex, we needed help. We both started reeducating ourselves about what a healthy sexual life could look like. We read books and listened to talks with sex-positive messaging.

Ultimately, first I needed to remember that *I am good*, with all my perceived inadequacies, sexual desires and fears. If we start in a place of wholeness and goodness, then we can accept all of ourselves first. We can know our own wants and desires as good and normal and part of our unique identity. Then we are able to give to our partner out of wholeness and not deficit. This creates the foundation of belonging, a belonging that must start with ourselves, knowing that the fullness of our sexual selves is invited to the table of love.

Next, I needed to not fear freedom. Freedom from the repression of my sexual self was terrifying. The only way I would be able to risk sharing myself fully was if I knew I had a partner who would be with me no matter what, unconditionally. I had to trust I was free to explore, question, imagine something more beautiful, more intimate, and more inclusive of all of me.

What we all desire is both safety and freedom. Safety and belonging with our partner are crucial for trust and intimacy. This mentality, I believe, is how sexual health will flourish.

The turnaround came in our sex life when we got fully honest about our past stories, current expectations, and future desires. You started believing that sex could be good for you and could be good for us. You finally allowed yourself to enjoy sex and it stopped being a chore.

**Yup, and I turned thirty-four.**

It was like a switch turned on. I could not keep up. It was the first time you started figuring out what felt good to you and what didn't. And most importantly, you started communicating those desires with me.

**And I stopped birth control and you got a vasectomy.**

I got a vasectomy and you got a toy. All the stars aligned. Once you can talk with each other about sex, then you can share what you want from each other. Remember when I made you look online to find a vibrator?

**Are we really going to talk about this?**

I think it was a turning point in our sex life. It normalized sex conversations for us. We literally looked at all different shapes and sizes. And I made you buy a vibrator right then and there.

**It was so embarrassing.**

Actually it was really funny. We laughed at the wide array of sex toys. It opened you up to new experiences and it created a fun way to talk about our likes and dislikes.

**We used to think these conversations were taboo or bad, but we learned from our sex therapist that women sometimes need a little help. Or in Laurie Watson's exact words, "Men are like gondolas and women have to climb the mountain."**

The safest place to talk about all this is with your lifelong partner. We all have different stories, drives, and desires, and we need to be able to communicate openly. Our conversation started awkward, became really funny, and ultimately opened ourselves to each other. Sometimes we have to push past what is uncomfortable to move toward what is vulnerable.

**That is true. It was a really funny conversation. Who would have thought that one sex toy purchase would bring more freedom to our entire sex life?**

I learned very quickly that trying new sexual experiences together was not "bad," it simply made sex better for you and in turn for me. Sex needs to stay exciting and we have to try new things continuously to keep things interesting and have a greater level of intimacy.

**That reminds me of the time you set up fifty candles around a pile of pillows on the living room floor.**

It started romantic, but it didn't turn out quite the way I imagined.

**It was great until one of the pillows caught on fire and my hair started smoking.**

You have to admit it was kinda funny. But honestly, to have a healthy sexual relationship we need to know our partner's desires and needs and mutually help each other meet those needs.

**What do you mean by that?**

Like how you prioritize our intimacy before I have to leave town for work.

**First of all, I hate how you say "intimacy." It's sex.**

Okay, let me say it a little more clearly. You and I have sex before I leave for work trips.

**Yes, I sense that travel is hard for you. I can tell it can make you feel disconnected from me.**

Work travel can be difficult for sexual health. Temptation seems to be compounded when couples separate. Especially for men (but in no way limited to men).

**I guess I know this instinctively and want to help us still feel connected even when we're not together.**

Work travel has caused too many relationships to fall apart. Practically speaking, sex before and after trips can really help, and we've talked openly and honestly about that.

**So how do we start these difficult and sometimes awkward conversations with our partner? There are so many fears and insecurities that block us from the conversations we need to have about sex. I often feared what you thought about our sex life (was it horrible?), about my body (was I sexy enough for you?), and about our intimacy (was it what you wanted?). Yet so much of sexiness is confidence! (And I clearly didn't have it.) Ultimately, I needed to know me. I needed to own and know my sexuality before I was able to fully connect with you.**

You might be reading this and thinking, "Jeff seems to have it all figured out and André had the problem." That is 100 percent not true. You see, I couldn't figure out what she wanted, which led to doubt about never being able to give her what she needed. If I couldn't give that to her, would she start finding it somewhere else? I thought I was the problem in our sex life. But really, neither of us was being fully honest out of fear of hurting the other.

**The problem was that we didn't have an open and continual dialogue about sex.**

You and your partner can't have a singular sex talk; you need regular open conversations. The more you talk about sex with your partner, the better sex will become. "Research shows that couples who can talk openly about sex have more sex, and the women in these relationships have more orgasms."[4]

Did I convince you? More sex and orgasms? Sign me up.

But one thing that sexologist Dr. Celeste Holbrook says is that sex is difficult to talk about for most people. We are never taught how to talk about sex. Sex is a "learned behavior," but no one is teaching us very well. This was true for me; learning to talk about sex was a slow, tortuous process. It was a forced extrication of my questions and thoughts about sex.

One bold, all-caps-worthy find: NO CRITICISM IN THE BEDROOM. EVER. Discussion during "sex time" should sound like, "I like it when you . . . ," or "It feels so good when you . . ." Outside of the bedroom, in a neutral conversational space, is where you should have discussions about what is or is not working well for you. (You're welcome for this "learned the hard way" tip!)

I think conversations about sex should happen not only with each other but also with your closest friends. I'm not saying you should share every intimate detail with every friend in your life, but your sex life can improve when you talk about it with your friends.

That is 100 percent true. It's funny, ever since our sex podcast aired, I have talked to more women about sex than ever before. I guess I just needed to say the three Vs (vulva, vagina, and vibrator) on air to get people talking! Victory—ah, make it four Vs. But the resounding message is the same: we all feel a little more normal when we talk about the hardships of our experiences around sex.

No doubt you've experienced at least one of these hardships and maybe more: infertility (when sex is a chore and scheduled around a calendar and then it doesn't "work" like it's supposed to), postpartum (when nothing about your vagina feels normal yet and your hormones are still crazy), menopause (when women lose estrogen and desire drops and nothing feels the same anymore), premature ejaculation (when sex is over too soon, resulting in embarrassment), and erectile dysfunction (the shame and struggle around this issue for men are real). And the list goes on.

These are conversations I have almost every single day with my patients. There are so many difficulties with sex drives, hormone changes, and medical and physical effects on sexuality and relationships. Sex is not easy. It changes through the years because of unavoidable bodily changes and unfortunate circumstances, which can lead to a lot of disappointment. Yet when we can talk honestly and share our experiences with someone, that, my friends, is the first step toward healing. One step toward knowing you are not alone in this world. There is healing no matter how disappointed you feel, no matter what your sex life looks like right now. Despite our sexual history, we can find freedom in our sexual health today.

Hearing our friends share some of their stories has opened more conversations for us. Sex talk has become less scary and way funnier. We've heard stories about hiding hickeys, having sex at the in-laws' house, getting frisky in store dressing rooms, trying thirty-day sex challenges, and figuring out what in the world to say when your kids walk in on you.

Sharing vulnerably with others creates more freedom and honesty in other relationships as well as our own. That's one more V we need to pay a lot of attention to as well: sex is *vulnerable*.

When you can't trust and feel safe, you can't have good sex. High trust and affection in a low-stress space creates the best atmosphere for good sex. It took me a long time to realize this. I mean, I barely tolerated my own body, let alone felt safe showing another person my naked body (ahem, shower curtain). How was I to trust another human being with my body? Would he judge me as much as I judged myself in my own head?

Vulnerability is about being willing to share your true self with your partner. Brené Brown describes it as "uncertainty, risk and emotional exposure."[5] Opening your inner world to the one person you are in a committed relationship with will enrich your sex life and take it to new levels. Can you share your fears, insecurities, wishes, and desires with your partner and know they will hold them carefully, gently, and with total acceptance? Or has a wall of hurt, abandonment, or rejection been built between you, causing a distancing of your hearts? When you stop being vulnerable with your partner, you stop being intentional with your partner. Are you going through the physical motions of sex but not connecting with open hearts? Have you stopped sharing your secrets with each other? Your partner should be your number one, your safe place, the one person you trust in your sexual world.

## HOW TO KEEP THE PASSION?

Marriage and sex therapist Esther Perel often says that responsibility is the biggest killer of arousal. Her observation explains why sexual energy is so hot in the beginning. Think about the beginning of your relationship when you burned for each other, could hardly keep your hands off each other, were always looking for the next moment you could be together (hoping it would include nakedness). Likely this was a time when you didn't have a lot of responsibilities. You might have had a job or school or rent, but really you were only responsible for yourself. Those were the good ol' days.

Now, most of you reading this book have way more responsibilities, like raising good humans who depend on you for everything! With kids, the responsibilities pile up quickly. It's not just the children; it's their school, their lunches, their doctor appointments, their activities, their grades, and their drama. And that doesn't even include our own adult appointments, work, volunteer activities, relationships, and drama. It all adds up to a monster truck load of responsibility.

To be honest, we don't carry it all on our shoulders; no, we keep it somewhere more dangerous: our minds. We carry a heavy mental load. All the pieces are scrambled up in our heads as we try to organize our lives and keep everything together. Staying on top of all our responsibilities takes a lot of mental energy. This is a major problem in our sexual health: the to-do list in our heads. I have a never-ending list in my head that I keep checking off and adding to. My mental list is hard to turn off and ultimately causes a lack of mental presence, and yet this presence is necessary to stay connected to myself and my partner. Research shows the most important factor for women in creating and sustaining a fulfilling sex life is not what you do in bed or how you do it but how you feel about it. *Presence.* Which means that stress, mood, trust, and body image are central contributors to women's sexual well-being.[6]

Sometimes you need to turn off that list in your brain so we can turn up the heat in bed. When "The List" takes over, we seem more like roommates than lovers.

**Yes, we know married couples who are very good roommates. They never fight. They work, shuffle**

**their kids to activities, and do all the normal family living. They are great parents, show up at every game, cook healthy dinners, play family games . . .**

But they don't have any sex. When your life together is centered around logistics, carpooling, task lists, and coparenting—this is the death of erotic sexual health.

**Did you just say erotic? Wow, you really went there. So what you're saying is that eroticism is dead when we let tasks take priority over sex?**

We had a friend tell us, "We created such a productive life that it was negatively impacting intimacy." I believe a lack of regular good sex is an indicator of a deeper marital tension.

**You've become roommates and not lovers.**

That would be a good question to ask ourselves to make sure we are sexually healthy: Are we good lovers, or are we better at being roommates?

In our *Love or Work* podcast with sex therapist Laurie Watson, she talked about the 4-4-4 Principle.[7] She emphasized the need for each partner to have four hours of autonomy each week and for both partners to have four hours of time together each week. These chunks of personal and together time allow each person to feel autonomous but also bring them back together. The time away is so essential for building desire. When Jeff comes back from his four hours, I'm intrigued and curious: What did you read about during your time away? What are you learning? What ideas are going through your head?

Also, ladies, I don't resent his being gone for four hours because I know I'm going to have my four hours too. Or if four hours is too difficult (e.g., you're breastfeeding every two hours), make the principle 2-2-2. It's hard to believe, but time apart can lead to increased connectedness as long as you are intentional about caring for yourself and your relationship.

Laurie also said that if couples had sex twice per week—in her words, "one quickie and one longie"—they wouldn't be in her office needing sex help.

**Jeff, I don't want this chapter to be prescriptive. I don't want to tell people how often they should have sex!**

I get that. And I want our readers to have more and better sex. This is not a prescription. I'm just reflecting on key principles we learned in our research.

**Well, in that case, sex should never be about quantity; it should always be about quality. [Wink]**

Who's being prescriptive now?

**Hey, I'm just trying to help women have more orgasms, that's all.**

## SEX AND WORK

As soon as I wrote those words (*sex*, *work*), I thought about the #MeToo movement and the misuse of power and sex in the workplace. This abuse is common and continues to be a problem, but we're not going to address that topic here. Much more qualified experts have shed light on the issue (see https://metoomvmt.org). What we want to talk about are the positive ways that sex can improve work and work can improve sex (*and* lead to more orgasms!). We had a great conversation on the *Love or Work* podcast with Cristina and Andy Mineo[8] about sex and work, and

I will never forget what Cristina said: "We can't ask women to break glass ceilings in work and they can't even ask for what they want in the bedroom." (Preach, sister!)

In our research, we found that a slight majority (57 percent) of adults believe working has a positive effect on their sex life, while 43 percent believe it has a negative effect. Sixty-one percent of men feel that working has a positive effect on their sex life, compared with 53 percent of women. Younger adults say working positively affects their sex life more than older adults.

We all know that sex releases endorphins that elevate our mood, help us relax, and make us feel more loving with our partner, but did you know sex can improve your work?

You had to know that in a book called *Love or Work* we were going to discuss *sex* and *work,* right? (No, not sex *at* work. Get your minds out of the gutter.)

In 2017 researchers[9] at Oregon State University followed 159 married couples working in a variety of industries (education, health care, retail, government, etc.) for two weeks and asked them two simple questions each morning: (1) How many times did they have sexual intercourse between the end of the work shift yesterday and right now? (2) On a scale of 1 to 5, what was the extent to which they felt the following emotions: inspired, alert, excited, enthusiastic, and determined? The employees who engaged in sex the previous evening reported more positive moods in the morning, which led to greater work engagement and job satisfaction. The effects were equally strong for men and women.

Crazy, huh? I guess sex does transcend the bedroom—now it's improving the boardroom!

Not only did this study show the positive effects of sex on work; conversely, the study suggested that bringing home work-related stress may impact our love life and work life. Ah, yes, this is where we all feel the tension. This is when we are too tired, too stressed, too overwhelmed for sex. The study found what we all know: that work brought home to the family caused conflict and reduced the likelihood of engaging in sex at home that evening. The authors wrote, "As the boundary between work and home life continues to erode through technology and increasing expectations of availability, employers would be wise to consider practices such as limiting urgent-response emails in the evening, when employees may be engaging in physical intimacy, which appears to positively affect work behavior the following day." (Basically, stop bothering your employees in the evening so they can *get it on*!)

In our own research, we asked participants if work positively or negatively affected their sex life and found that 61 percent of men and 53 percent of women thought work positively affected their sex life. Women seemed to be more dissatisfied than men. When we pushed further to ask about areas of dissatisfaction in life, women, more than men, were dissatisfied with the amount of sleep, exercise, and stress in their lives.

Science supports the idea that stress negatively impacts your sex life. Elevated stress over a long period of time starts to raise cortisol levels in your blood, which then blocks the production of testosterone. Testosterone is the sex hormone that affects sex drive in both men and women. Low testosterone = low sex drive. All these chemical changes are happening in our bodies, and we don't even realize it!

Science also supports the idea that sex positively impacts your work life.

You experience an improved focus level and increased productivity the day after you have sex. So if you're trying to get something done, you might want to start with sex first.

**That seems like a weird reason for sex.**

It is a little weird. But honestly, when I'm stressed, I often start separating myself from you—when in reality I should be connecting with you.

**Stress often causes us to isolate ourselves, to retreat inward. This withdrawal from our partner causes even more strain on the relationship. Do you see the cycle?**

This is me one hundred percent. I get stressed about something at work, and then I go inward in my thoughts and pull away from you. When really I probably need you the most during these times.

**Yeah, I see that. My stress amps up my "fight or flight" mode, and I tend to fight or get snappy or irritated with you quickly.**

When you break me out of my own thoughts and ask me to share them with you, it helps a lot. It opens up communication and allows me to vent.

**What helps me is when you remind me we're on the same team and ask me if there is anything you can do to help me carry the load.**

It also helps when you initiate sex when I'm stressed. Sex is the best stress reliever.

**Ha-ha. Okay, babe, I'll remember that.**

Let's go back and remember the important stuff. Dive into your past and take note of the positive or negative experiences that have impacted your current view of sex. Talk about those issues with your partner so you both can understand each other's viewpoint. Remember that sex is good and sexual health is important for everyone, and have conversations regularly with each other and close friends. Help each other find time for autonomy so that you can connect in a more meaningful and vulnerable way. Finally, don't forget another great bonus: sex improves your work engagement! So don't give up. Your sex life can be great, even if it's not right now. And if it's great, we bet talking through some of the questions below with your partner will make it even better.

Next we'll talk about the kids we are raising and the good humans we hope they will become.

## TALK ABOUT IT

Before you move forward, take a moment to answer these questions on your own and invite your partner to discuss them with you.

1. Do you talk about sex? To your partner? To your friends? Who are the friends you feel most comfortable talking about sex with? If you don't talk about sex with others, why not?
2. Do you know what you like? Share with your partner your favorite sexual experience you have ever had together and a new experience you want to try next.
3. When you or your partner travels, what are ways you can try to stay connected emotionally and intimately?
4. Share your sexual history with each other. How did you learn about sex? Have your past experiences been mostly positive or negative? Why were they good or bad?

## DO A CHALLENGE

We all need creative ideas for taking what we read and putting it into practice. Share your experience with others and tag @loveorwork #loveorwork.

***Spice things up.*** In this chapter we talked about many things that could be good for your sex life. Talk with your partner about trying something new! We know this discussion might be scary, but it could also bring greater freedom and openness. You might want to try a new location. You might want to try a new position. You might want to buy a toy together or try a sex question game to spice things up. Explore something new together.

## LISTEN UP

Add to this journey by listening to a free podcast that relates to this chapter and will give you even more to process. Go to www.loveorwork.com/listenup.

**Sex Therapy with an Expert: Laurie Watson (Episode 42)**

To hear an open and honest conversation covering a broad range of questions about sex, listen to expert sex therapist Laurie Watson answer each question with candor. She is author of the book *Wanting Sex Again: How to Rediscover Your Desire and Heal a Sexless Marriage* and cohost of the podcast *Foreplay: Radio Sex Therapy*.

the CHARACTER of our CHILDREN is MORE IMPORTANT than THEIR CULTURAL SUCCESS.

-ANDRÉ SHINABARGER-

#LOVE or WORK

CHAPTER 10

# *Raising Humans*

## ANDRÉ

**It is not what you do for your children, but what you have taught them to do for themselves, that will make them successful human beings.**

—ANN LANDERS

One of our biggest fights in marriage was about how we were going to raise our son.

At this point in time, our son was three years old and had a five-year-old sister who loved princesses and dancing and all things sparkly. Naturally, our boy wanted to be like his sister and followed suit. He leaped around the house in tutus regularly, danced in heels (while wearing his Iron Man mask), and loved to paint his nails pink. Our boy was eccentric, creative, and, some would say, feminine. This brought some tension to our family—well, mostly between Jeff and me. Our fight played out like this:

André, you need to stop encouraging
Neko when he's acting "girly."

**Acting "girly"? [Said with huge air quotes and all the sass I could muster up] What do you mean by that?**

I mean, you regularly paint his nails pink!

**He asks me to paint his nails pink!**

He is going to get mocked and laughed at by his friends at school. Don't you care about that?

**He is three years old! If his friends say something, we'll figure it out. It's not that big of a deal. If we make it a big deal, then it becomes a big deal. If we don't, then it won't!**

Not that big of a deal? Kids are mean, André—you have to know that. One day he's going to be traumatized by his pink nails—that you painted—and then what?

**Listen, I showed him all the colors, and he chose pink!**

## RAISING SONS WHO RESPECT WOMEN

Three years later, our son's favorite color is "rainbow" and he still loves to paint his nails. He is emotional and sensitive and adores his older sister. These are wonderful traits I love about his character. Yet I sometimes wonder, should I encourage him to be manlier, tougher? Should I work on promoting his masculinity? Will that help him survive the macho culture we live in today?

This is what I know to be true about my son: He is brave. He is courageous, because even though students at school tease him about his nail polish, he still asks me to paint his nails. He knows mean kids will say stupid stuff, and he walks out the door rocking his painted nails with his head held high because he really, really likes pink. There is a rich beauty in both the feminine and masculine qualities in all people, and we all carry both qualities inside us. We carry *human* qualities inside us.

There are spectrums of masculinity and femininity inside everyone. Some of us have a little more of one or the other, and this is part of what makes each of us unique. I was considered a tomboy growing up. I loved playing sports and constantly tried to beat the boys to show them a girl could ball better than they could. I hated dresses (don't even get me started on tights—can I get an amen?), never wore makeup, and was convinced that whatever a boy could do I would do better. I wonder if my parents were ever concerned about me. I wonder if they thought my "unwomanly" ways would impede my future. Did they worry I would never attract a husband? Would I have only boys as friends and never develop true friendships with women? Would I ever have a sleepover with my girlfriends and talk about boys? Would I be too "butch"? Would I be a lesbian?

Let's return to our fight about Neko and the rabbit hole of our own parenting questions.

The conversation began to shift as we realized we were talking about the superficial outward actions of our boy instead of looking at the real fears we had as parents.

**Jeff, I think this is about more than nail polish and tutus.**

I agree, but I can't articulate what bothers me so much.

**I think it's based on unconscious expectations we have of our kids. Maybe fears of what this means he might become when he is older.**

I think that's true. I imagined him playing sports like I did. I imagined him to be more boyish. But I also hope he is extremely creative. I don't want him to be fearful of what others think. André, what if he is gay? Not that being gay is wrong or bad, but I can't imagine how hard that could be for him one day, especially in this hateful society where being gay is still marginalized . . . and that breaks my heart. The truth is I wanted my son to be just like me, and the reality is, he is wonderfully different.

This. This was the root of it. The root of all we had been fighting about. It wasn't about the polish, ruffles, and sparkles. There's a common confusion (dare we call it fear?) among parents about where their children land on the masculine/feminine spectrum and how this will impact their future. And it's the unknown future part that worries parents the most.

We all want the best for our children. We want to protect them. We want life to be safe and love-filled for our family, our community, and the larger society. And what we also know from historical events, current events, and many of our own gay friends is that love outside the mainstream box often means oppression, inequality, and injustice. Deep down, Jeff's fear is that this "feminine" quality of our son's personality might translate to a battle with society's hatefulness. One of our greatest fears is that our children will be marginalized, bullied, shamed, or—worse—attacked when we're not there to protect them.

Loving your children while working on your parenting is not easy. Sometimes it means that a fight about rainbow-painted nails leaves you with a responsibility to fight for a society that can do better for our children. You were a child once. Chances are, you felt the bruise of landing outside of the cushy majority. Were you a tomboy? Were you uninterested in sports? Were you always wishing you carried a little less weight? Were you labeled the "dumb jock"? Were you more interested in books than people? Were you trying to find your way in a world where you didn't always fit? All these idiosyncrasies in our beings caused pain and confusion in some way when we were kids. We felt the mocking and teasing. And we'd do anything to protect our children from that. Right? We don't want them to feel anything but happy and confident to be exactly who they are.

We want our kids to be everything they want to be, do everything they want to do, and feel fully alive. Why is it that the dreams of our children have no glass ceiling, but in society there are limitations on what is possible in the workplace? Parents, we have work to do. We can and should be part of shattering the "power ceilings" in society that box in our children based on gender, color, sexuality, or identity. How we raise our kids, love our partner, and do our work shows what we believe about ceilings. It shows our kids whether we believe in their dreams and their potential. Turns out, loving children is work.

And then our kids throw us another plot twist: Hey, Mom. Hi, Dad. Quick chat: I'm not you. I'm not going to be exactly like you. I might not even be what you consider "normal."

(Sigh.)

Kids.

Kids are weird.

But the truth is that we need to accept them (dare we say celebrate them?) in all that weirdness if we really want them to be all they can be. Our hard lesson with Neko was learning that if we want him to be fully himself, then we have to stop shuffling him along the path of cultural masculinity we thought would protect him.

How many of you reading this want a man who will be sensitive to your feelings, who will cry and show his emotions if he is upset, and who will gently nurture the kids when they act like little punks? A man who knows and understands his feelings is so attractive. I love seeing that side of Jeff. I love the vulnerability and connection we have in those moments. If we are honest about that, then maybe we can open space to validate both femininity and masculinity as beautiful and even essential in the boys (and girls) we are raising. I read an interesting study that compared the words *compassionate* and *caring* between men and women.[1] These two words were considered positive traits for women but were seen more negatively for men. I disagree.

When I think of raising a boy, one of the most important traits I want him to learn is respect for women. We have all seen the news stories about men in power mistreating women. This abuse stems from a toxic masculinity that tells boys to hide their emotions and encourages toughness, strength, and force. Yet when the open expression of feelings is prohibited and emotions get shoved down, one day those emotions erupt—and the eruption causes destruction to oneself and often to others. Psychologists say a man with no emotional outlets will unleash his repressed anger on those who are deemed weaker, different, or more feminine. In fact, it's not just toxic masculinity we need to be aware of in our work as parents; the American Psychological Association (the smartest people on mental health) says that traditional masculinity is toxic and encouraging boys not to cry is dangerous to their health.[2]

Uh-oh, I told my kids last week to "suck it up" and to "stop crying because I don't want to hear it."

As parents, we all make these mistakes. *We just want to stop the whining!* However, after reading every single page of the updated APA guidelines, my eyes are open to the ways I have repressed my son's (and daughter's) emotions at times. I think the point here is that we as parents need to be aware. It takes work to be aware. It takes love too.

If I'm honest, I don't want to hear my kids' feelings most of the time. I am so bad at this. I constantly find myself saying, "I don't want to hear it" (my go-to phrase when they have some "reasonable" explanation). Now I try to catch myself and say, "I *do* want to hear it. I want to hear how you feel about what just happened." And then I shut up and listen. This has been my new practice, my new work, out of love. This is my first step toward change.

Another study revealed that boys ages ten to nineteen say "strength" and "toughness" are the male character traits most valued by society.[3] Daniel Goleman, author of *Emotional Intelligence*, says, "Family life is our first school for emotional learning."[4] Reflecting on Goleman's observation led me to some deeper questions I wanted to ask Jeff.

**Jeff, do you think you need to be tough and strong for me?**

No. You definitely are strong enough for both of us.

**Well then, what do you think society told you a man should be for a woman?**

The protector and provider for the family.

**Ah, yes.**

It's kind of laughable in our scenario.

**Why?**

Well, it's another false narrative. It's another way for men to feel superior.

Who do men need to provide for and protect? Who is the weaker one? This idea sets up an inequality. This idea imprints into men's brains and subtly suggests that they must be stronger than someone else. Let's raise boys who become men who fully respect and love women well and equally. It starts with rejecting masculine[5] and feminine stereotypes and then showing them that girls and women are their equals and deserve honor and respect, showing our sons that we are all humans. We don't know the rest of Neko's story yet. A year later and Neko has gone from loving tutus to magic tricks. What we do know is that we will love him. Period.

## RAISING DAUGHTERS WHO RESPECT THEMSELVES

**What's the greatest lesson a woman should learn?**
**That since day one**
**She's already had everything she needs within herself.**
**It's the world that convinced her she did not.**

—RUPI KAUR

It's fascinating how we often raise our kids differently depending on their gender. One father told me he never really thought about what his boys thought about women, or their mother, until he had a baby girl. Suddenly, he began thinking about his daughter's future and determined that he wanted his daughter to know she could be and do anything. Then he realized his wife, the mother of his new baby girl, would be the one she watched closely and wanted to emulate. Just as the boys looked up to their father, so the girl would look up to her mother. Yet it wasn't until he had a daughter that he thought about what she would see in her mother.

I often wonder what my daughter notices about me. Here are glimpses into conversations with my daughter that tell me how she sees me:

**Me:** (putting on makeup at the bathroom sink)
**Her:** Mommy, why do you think you need makeup?
**Me:** (*Oh no, I'm not ready for this conversation! Don't say "to cover my flaws."*) Well, baby, because I just want to accentuate my pretty eyelashes and cheekbones.
**Her:** Didn't you say God made us beautiful just as we are?
**Me:** Uh . . . well, yeah.

Another day:

> **Her:** Mommy, why are you straightening your hair? You have pretty natural waves. Didn't you tell me that my natural curls are gorgeous?
>
> **Me:** (Sigh. *Good point.*)

The point is: I didn't have an answer.

She is watching me. Watching what I prioritize. Watching what I get upset about. She hears me when I talk about other women. Am I critical or am I kind? She hears the things I say about myself. Am I critical or am I kind? Does she hear negativity about my body? Do I talk about being too jiggly and needing to diet? Soon she will be a teenager staring at herself in the mirror. Will she repeat those same phrases to herself?

I am not "mother blaming" anyone. I don't believe all mothers do this, and I don't believe parents who have teenagers struggling with self-image are at fault. There are so many external pressures and demands outside of the home that affect our children. We can't cover their eyes from the magazines at the grocery store checkout. We can't prevent girls from being told they need to "look better" in this society. But we do need to admit our mistakes and encourage body positivity in our children. If we can be honest about our own woundedness and learn to accept those areas we dislike about ourselves, we can help our daughters become confident as well. It is hard work; a labor of love.

Women, we face so many societal and professional pressures and expectations to look and act a certain way. Receiving these mixed messages every day telling us how to act and behave can make us feel like we're in the movie *Groundhog Day*, repeating the same script again and again.

We need to be sexy but not slutty;
we need to be professional but not a prude;

we need to be engaging but not wild;
we need to be serious but not a downer;
we need to be competitive but not emotional;
we need to dream big but not demand;
we need to be outgoing but not loud;
we need to be kind but not an airhead;
we need to be smart but not challenging;
we need to be strong but not bossy;
we need to take initiative but not rock the boat.

Women, no doubt you can add your own "need to be __________ but not __________" that's been thrown at you on the daily as well.

Are you as confused as I am about the prototype woman our society values? What are we telling our daughters?

How do we learn to love ourselves and our bodies, exactly as we are right now? Hillary McBride, author of *Mothers, Daughters, and Body Image: Learning to Love Ourselves as We Are*, says we need to learn self-compassion and we need to be able to say our body is okay at any size. Isn't this a truth we want to pass along to our daughters? But how do we suddenly become okay with our thick thighs and saggy triceps? Hillary, when interviewed in a podcast,[6] said, "You can believe that and start acting like it, or you could act like it and then you'll believe it later." I have fallen into the latter category.

After the makeup incident with my daughter, I decided I was ditching makeup (for a short period of time or forever, I wasn't sure). I wanted to challenge myself, to see if I could still love myself in my "natural element." Everything inside me cringed at the bags under my eyes. I desperately wanted to add some cover-up and mascara to help me look more awake. Yet I really wanted to experiment and see if I could shatter the lie that I needed makeup to look beautiful—a lie I didn't want my daughter growing up believing.

As I started this experiment, I did not feel beautiful or believe I was either, so I clung to my defiant and determined spirit and "acted out" that confidence. And I am here to tell you, promise you, it worked! Not all the time and not every day, but that certainty in myself without any cover-up became mostly true. Once, when we traveled, I forgot my makeup bag and managed not to panic. (I know most of you women know that feeling.) I also observed Jeff did not once notice. He never asked or said a word about my lack of makeup, and his actions toward me never changed. I was fully and wholly accepted. This experiment freed me from the chains that said, "You are prettier with makeup."

A year later, I occasionally use cosmetics (it's still fun to dress up and wear that red lipstick sometimes), but to be honest, most days I forget to apply anything, and the most important part is that I feel free. This is the freedom I want for our daughters, freedom to be completely themselves.

Do I dare take this one step further? I would like to propose moving beyond body positivity to body neutrality. Lindsay and Lexie Kite, who run a nonprofit promoting body image resilience called Beauty Redefined, have been amazing teachers on this topic.[7] They say that "body neutrality isn't just thinking you are beautiful; it is knowing you are more than beautiful." They remind us that loving your body isn't just about believing you look good; it's knowing *your body is good no matter how it looks*. Body neutrality is a reminder that our bodies are instruments for our use, not adornments for others to admire.[8]

Mic drop! If women start believing this idea, what a change we could make to the diet industry and the cosmetic industry. So much of our energy (and money) goes toward "fixing" ourselves! Can you imagine the impact on the next generation if we lived like we believe our worth is more than our appearance? I get goose bumps just thinking about the revolution that could happen.

Another way to get free is to lift up women making an impact. I want my daughter to see how women support each other instead of falling into criticism and comparison. Tara Mohr, author of *Playing Big: Practical Wisdom for Women Who Want to Speak Up, Create, and Lead*, talks about why women criticize each other so harshly. "It rattles us to see in them (other women) what we have not permitted in ourselves."[9] Think about that. It's not them; it's us. We don't feel empowered ourselves, so we are critical and judgy of women who do seem empowered. Our insecurities only grow as we deny our own dreams and treat ourselves harshly. Mohr talks about every woman working on her own self, "playing big" by giving herself full permission to pursue her passions and dreams, because when she is becoming the woman she longs to be, she can be supportive of other women doing so as well. Don't we want daughters who find the good in others? Don't we want daughters who avoid gossip and choose kindness over critique?

Which leads to another big trouble area we all fall into: comparison.

We spend so much time looking outward, comparing someone's staged perfection on social media to our brutal real-life moments. When I see a model's perfected image in a photo shoot and compare myself, I forget a few important facts. First, modeling is her job. She did not just work ten hours at the clinic, rush to pick up the kids, then quickly smile pretty for a photo. She also did not just walk onto the set. She literally sat for hours in a chair while at least six staff members finessed every pore and strand of hair to perfection prior to this shot. Not to mention the edits and airbrushes.

I know you know this. But we have to *remember* this!

This is what Sarah Dubbeldam, founder of *Darling* magazine, calls "media literacy."[10] This is why we cannot compare our current state (which right now is me in Jeff's huge Michigan State sweatpants and fuzzy slippers, with crazy hair that has not been touched in twenty-four hours) with the photoshopped, filtered images we see on Instagram. This kind of comparison causes us to feel defeated, discouraged, and discontent. We need to free ourselves and our daughters from this misconception about real beauty.

How can we avoid the comparison trap and help our daughters stop the exhausting cycle? The insights I've gathered have convinced me one important way is reminding myself of my own purpose. Remembering my significance in my own lane helps me keep my comparison tendencies in check. No one can do what you do with your specific work, with your beautiful family, with your current relationships. They are uniquely yours in this time and place in the world. When I remember that my lane matters, the other lanes around me (which I keep comparing myself to) start to fade in significance, like the portrait mode on your iPhone that zeroes in on the subject in view as the surrounding secondary details blur. This is your one life! When you continue to compare your life with the lives around you, you diminish the importance of this precious life and you lose focus. This is the gift we can give our daughters every day. We can remind them of their lane—their strengths and their uniqueness. We can help them break free of comparisons and remind them to enjoy this one beautiful life they have been given.

"Okay, André, but my life is not so great right now." I hear you, friends. You are in it. This is the fire, the test for true gold. It is also the time when you can choose how to respond. Will you lean into this rough patch and find beauty? Can you find the good in this darkness? When I've been in these dark spaces in my marriage, in my work life, in my spiritual walk, in my parenting, gratitude has been my lifeline. When I feel like I'm drowning as the waves crash around me, every act and spoken word of thankfulness has been like a strong pull of my body one arm's length further along the life rope toward the shore of joy. Ann Voskamp writes, "Being joyful isn't what makes you grateful. Being grateful is what makes you joyful."[11]

Right here. Right now.

In the midst of all the chaos, I know there is light; there are those small moments of joy we cling to and remember as significant. This is what I want our daughters to see us doing: clinging to moments of joy, honoring the good during the hard. Brené Brown says, "Joy comes to us in moments—ordinary moments. We risk missing out on joy when we get too busy chasing down the extraordinary."[12]

Here is where I see comparison discrediting the beautiful ordinary moments. We believe the lie that the Hollywood actress is living an extraordinary life and that her life is somehow *more*. Is it? Is her life more valuable? We know it isn't, and yet we somehow seem to forget that truth. Young children are so helpful in reminding us of the importance of presence. They teach us to live in the moment. If you watch young kids, you'll see they have no concept of the future, no idea that something could be better than what is right now. They live in full joy and wild abandon each moment.

May we be like our beautiful children and see the good. May our love of our daughters be so strong and fierce that they grow up with no self-imposed restrictions on who they can be. May we raise daughters who love themselves fully, grounded in who they are and ready to fly.

## RAISING GOOD HUMANS

What if we flipped the script and shifted the paradigm of raising sons and daughters? What if we focused on raising good humans? We already know there are masculine and feminine qualities in everyone. What if we stop elevating one quality as superior in males or females? Maybe, just maybe, if we did the hard work of love and began seeing our kids as little humans slowly transitioning into adult humans—whom we adequately prepare for the big world without Mom and Dad—they would thrive.

Leadership guru Andy Stanley says his goal is to raise children who want to be with their parents and with each other when they no longer have to be.[13]

That's it: humans who want to be with you one day. The love and work of raising humans is not about managing or modifying behavior but about nurturing healthy relationships. Healthy relationships with others and with us is the goal when our kids become adults.

And what is a good human? From our learnings, we narrowed it down to these key principles:

- A good human knows and accepts who they are fully;
- A good human believes they can always grow and mature;
- A good human believes in the good of others around them;
- A good human treats all people with love, equity, and respect;
- A good human understands they have a unique purpose.

Here is the crux: we need to remember that the character of our children is more important than our society's version of success. Our family unit is more important than we can ever imagine, and our kids need to establish their identity in that safe place. Jeff's and my tiff about nail polish and tutus helped us peel back the layers of what it means to raise good humans and helped us dig down to what our son and daughter ultimately need from parents who love them deeply. Our kids—all kids—need a home and family more than any other thing. So much can be learned about life through sports: teamwork, body awareness, emotional control, and perseverance to name a few. But let's all give ourselves a hall pass for not shuffling our kids from one sport to the next every night of the week to instill those characteristics.

Creating opportunities for the success of our children is admirable; however, our kids might not succeed without the above fundamentals of being a good human. So maybe instead of focusing on good grades and the best schools, colleges, internships, and jobs, we can rest and believe that our children *will* get to those places, in their own unique way, as good humans. Along the way, what our *kids* want and need the most is simply our presence.

This approach frees us to focus on raising kids who pursue their passions with kindness, bravery, and determination. The key words here are "their passions," not our choices for them. Their passion might be baking, crafting, sports, chess club, puzzles, card tricks, or joke telling. Their passion might not fit into our box, and it might be something far outside our comfort zone. The point is, the specific passion doesn't matter as long as it is theirs.

In fact, the things our kids love will likely be far outside the realm of what we would choose for them. Katie Hurley, a child and adolescent psychotherapist, tackles the critical issue of passion in her book *The Happy Kid Handbook*. She writes that passion is a source of interest and excitement that is unique to each individual, and it can shift and change as kids grow. She adds that passion is not a trajectory for a successful life and it can't be forced. I guarantee those kids who know and pursue their passions will be world changers. Our job is to help our kids become the best versions of themselves, that is, good humans.

There is no one way to be a family and no one way to grow good humans. Raising children is about love and work. It is about the hard work of understanding yourself, your unconscious expectations, your gifts, your capacity, your family, and the need to make love-filled decisions that are right for your family. You will never be a perfect parent. You will never get it right every time. Parenting is a lot of trial and error. It's fights about nail polish, decisions about makeup, and a lot of mistakes (so many mistakes!). But they lead you to understanding what it truly means to raise good humans.

So let this collected wisdom encourage you to let go of what you think you know and what you think your kids should be, and grab onto a greater sense of freedom in your parenting. Set your kids free to be whoever they are created to be. And along the way, get other people involved in their lives. Read on to explore the importance of creating a village in the next chapter.

## TALK ABOUT IT

Before you move forward, take a moment to answer these questions on your own and invite your partner to discuss them with you.

1. In raising good humans, what is one distinct way you want to raise your kids differently than the way you were taught growing up?
2. Do you agree or disagree with the feminine and masculine perceptions that exist in our culture? How does that affect the way you choose to raise your children?
3. Do you relate to the pressures of being a woman or a man and the responsibilities that people put on you? How does that impact the way you're raising good humans?

4. Do you feel you have placed unconscious expectations on your children? If so, what are they? Do they stem from something you missed or loved in your own childhood?

## DO A CHALLENGE

We all need creative ideas for taking what we read and putting it into practice. Share your experience with others and tag @loveorwork #loveorwork.

***Write a letter to yourself.*** One thing we learned from the conversation between Jada and André is that our kids learn based on what they see modeled. Take a moment to write a letter and tell yourself what you love about yourself. Then write what you hope the next generation will replicate. Share the letter with your partner. If this exercise is difficult for you, ask your partner to join you; write a letter to each other and list what you see as meaningful qualities in the other person.

## LISTEN UP

Add to this journey by listening to a free podcast that relates to this chapter and will give you even more to process. Go to www.loveorwork.com/listenup.

### Becoming Better Grownups: Kristi and Brad Montague (Episode 88)

If you want to learn more about how to include your family in your work and raise good humans with big dreams, then listen to Kristi and Brad Montague's podcast. Brad is a *New York Times* bestselling author, and they cocreated Kid President, one of the most inspiring and successful YouTube channels. He also wrote the book *Becoming Better Grownups: Rediscovering What Matters and Remembering How to Fly.* Learn about how they have integrated their family into traveling to the White House and speaking on national morning talk shows. They believe in being a voice for good together as a family.

Our families will only be as loving as the collective love of our community.

-André Shimabarger-
#LOVE or WORK

CHAPTER 11

# *It Takes a Village*

## ANDRÉ

**Human beings need three basic things in order to be content: they need to feel competent at what they do; they need to feel authentic in their lives; and they need to feel connected to others.**

—SEBASTIAN JUNGER

"Jeff! I just got the phone call! This could be our baby!"

"What? So soon? Was the baby born?"

"Yes, the social worker just called—she's a girl, born eight days ago and ready for us to pick her up on Monday. We just need to say yes!"

"What? Three days?"

"Exactly! She's a preemie but healthy. I'm so excited. We are having a girl! What do you want to name her?"

"Umm . . . [Lots of stuttering] I just need a minute. Can I call you back? This is just so fast and so soon. I don't know if we can do this."

**"Oh, we are doing this. I read the bio of the birth mom. She chose us, everything checks out, the baby is healthy. I wonder what she looks like. It said her birth parents are tall—maybe she'll play basketball? Okay, I gotta go because I'm at work and have a ton more patients to see. Just text me some girl name ideas, okay?"**

"Uh, okay. Girl names. Got it . . . Wait! What did you read? Can you send me what they sent you? So I'm a dad now?"

**"Yes, babe, this is it! This is the adoption we've been planning and waiting for. This is our time."**

There were no months of preparation for us. That night we stared at each other in disbelief. We had zero baby things. There we sat with eyes wide, hearts full, tears flowing. We were so excited and terrified and had no idea what to do.

Jeff and I didn't know how else to announce our new baby coming in two days, so we did what everyone would do in those days and updated our status on Facebook: "We are going to be parents! Little Jada Rae is arriving in two days!"

The response of our community of friends and family was overwhelming. I had no clue what to register for (what's a wipe warmer, and do you really need one?), besides all the tiny human clothes and blankets (every baby needs blankets, right?). My friend Katie took charge and, unbeknownst to me, started organizing our friend group in purchasing all the necessities. We came home from work that day and noticed our porch was bursting with baby stuff: a crib, an infant car seat, boxes from Amazon, a baby swing. What in the world? How did this happen?

In two days, we had everything a baby human needs to survive.

Our *village* showed up.

## FRAMILY

Our village of friends without kids saved me. They were fresh and not sleep deprived. They were the ones who stepped in to make sure I was alive and eating and still remembering to have fun. They dragged me out for coffee, they brought food and wine, they reminded me to put on a bra, and they talked about anything else besides poop and feedings. These women were my life support. They brought oxygen to my zombie self that was barely sleeping and staying in pajamas with spit-up stains all day. These are the friends who become framily.

As Jada has grown older, these sweet friends have been her second mothers and favorite people. Jen Hatmaker calls these amazing women "bonus moms," and I couldn't agree more. These women have folded my children into their lives and encouraged and supported my kids at times when I couldn't. My daughter is a stronger and better person because they have invested in her in ways that I can't.

The village brings additional character building to the family, and, I would argue, it fosters greater personal growth than the sole family unit alone can provide.

My friend Katie and I have raised our children together for the last twelve years. She had a baby three years before me. I remember many nights of her walking through the door of our house with her screaming baby in outstretched arms. She would hand the baby straight to me and march to the kitchen to grab a glass of wine. I would then take her sweet screaming girl to the other room where I bounced with her on an exercise ball for hours to soothe her to sleep. It was our system, and it worked.

Katie had been walking and bouncing and dealing with the tears all day long; it was my turn to take her load. Years later after I had a baby girl, Katie became my child-care savior and offered to watch my baby while I worked. She helped carry my burden of being a working mom. We have taken turns supporting each other through all the ups and downs of parenting. Twelve years later, she is still "Mama Kate."

Annie is a twenty-year friend who moved to Atlanta to watch Neko when I went back to work. Her sacrifice to move and help me raise my children has been one of the most impactful examples of love to me and my family. When we didn't need "Annie the Nanny" regularly anymore, she told us she didn't want to be the "babysitter" or the "nanny." She wanted to hang out with our kids weekly and give us time once a week to have a date night. For five years she has loved our children weekly while Jeff and I take some much-needed time alone. I doubt our marriage would have survived without this contribution from a close friend. She is a part of our village who has taught our kids so much. She is a creative spirit who loves building projects. One summer she built a rainbow tree fort with Neko and a table with Jada, as well as teaching them both about veganism. These are things I could never teach them. I have never used a jigsaw in my life, and I eat meat. Annie has filled their lives with a creative energy that Jeff and I could never duplicate.

*The village extends our own personal capabilities and enhances the life of each person in the family.*

We want our kids to have mentors, safe people to talk to, whom we trust. Our kids need to feel loved and supported by adults who will encourage and teach them in ways we can't as parents. Our friends Chris and Teri own a beautiful lake house and have taken our kids to the lake on numerous occasions just to have special lake time.[1] Jada and Neko often return from their getaway weekends telling us stories of catching catfish, shooting a bow and arrows, or capturing frogs without squishing them (very important)—all things this city girl could not teach them (I shudder at the thought of slimy frogs). What a gift that someone else in our village can teach our kids aspects of life that we can't.

There is the informal village that we call framily, people you hang out with regularly, who love your kids because they are a part of you and don't expect anything in return. And then there is the formal village, those you pay to help you because you can't do everything. Those you pay for childcare, to clean the house, or to launder your clothes. In our research we were shocked to discover that 39 percent of our respondents have no formal village! They have no outside help. That means all the responsibilities of life, all the requirements of every day, rest solely on two people.

Yes, paying for extra help is a privilege; couples must have the finances for this possibility. Hiring a house cleaner, nanny, or babysitter can be costly. However, the informal village, your real-life friends, comes at no cost. This is where you can be creative with sharing costs among your community. Your village can step in and help with childcare like my friends Annie and Katie did, but there are also other practical ways the village can come together to help navigate life. Years ago, Jeff and I and many in our friend group were trying to pay off debt. We all made a pact that we would tackle this problem together. We realized that if we could be honest with our friends about our financial issues, then maybe we wouldn't feel so guilty about saying no to invitations that involved spending money. As a first step, we decided we would give up going out to dinner together and instead have "framily potlucks" at each other's houses. This way, no one felt left out if they couldn't afford dinners out. The potluck plan also encouraged us to be thoughtful of each other's financial situations and find ways to help each other. We could share resources and needs without embarrassment.

*When you know the needs in your community, finding ways to help each other is a gift for those giving and those receiving.*

Yet so often we don't trust others. Or maybe we do trust a ton of people; we just don't know how to ask for help and don't want to cut into others' precious time. In forgetting ourselves and not asking for help, are we forgetting each other? American culture is a culture of individualism, and it causes us to forget each other. We have forgotten our need for each other.

## WHY A VILLAGE IS TOUGH

Sebastian Junger, author of *Tribe*, explains how the village problem started. He says,

> First agriculture, and then industry, changed two fundamental things about the human experience. The accumulation of personal property allowed people to make more and more individualistic choices about their lives, and those choices unavoidably diminished group efforts toward a common good. And as society modernized, people found themselves able to live independently from any communal group. A person living in a modern city or a suburb can, for the first time in history, go through an entire day—or an entire life—mostly encountering complete strangers. They can be surrounded by others and yet feel deeply, dangerously alone. The evidence that this is hard on us is overwhelming.[2]

This sense of aloneness is the crux of the problem. The new mom feels alone and doesn't know how to ask for help. The neighbors seem busy, so you don't ask them over for dinner. All your friends have "stuff going on" that's more important than what you need, so you *feel* alone. These scenarios and so many more serve to disconnect us from others.

### We Are Individuals

Our society prides itself on individualism. We believe that we have the right to choose for ourselves what is good, what we need, and what we want and then make it happen. We believe in uniqueness, self-sufficiency, autonomy, and independence. We should be able to solve problems and accomplish goals on our own without having to rely on assistance from others, as in the old phrase "pull yourself up by your bootstraps." Though some parts of this viewpoint are helpful, I believe our individualistic culture has taken it too far. Even Pope Francis has acknowledged that our Western culture "has exalted the individual to the point of making him an island, almost as if one could be happy on one's own."[3]

We'd do well to learn from collectivist cultures, which focus on interdependent relationships more than the individual. In fact, the "village mentality" was founded by these cultures in Asia, Central and South America, and Africa. In these cultures, relationships and interconnectedness with others play a central role in each person's identity. People work together as a group to support each other. People are encouraged to do what is best for the whole instead of just themselves, and families and communities play a central role in society. Another key factor in collectivist cultures is low relational mobility, which means people's relationships are determined more by family and geographical area than by personal choice. Their relationships tend to be stable, strong, and long-lasting because they don't have the capability of meeting a lot of new people. Maybe we need more of a collectivist mentality in our families and villages? More focus on the success of the whole village and less focus on individual success?

### We Isolate

Isn't it crazy how we can go through an entire day without talking to or even seeing our neighbors? We walk out of our house through the garage, get in our car, drive to work, and drive back home straight into our garage. We can stay as isolated as we want. As Sebastian Junger says, we "can be surrounded by others and yet feel deeply, dangerously alone."

In 2017 many news headlines announced the "loneliness epidemic" as the national health crisis of our time. It is reported that two in five Americans say they sometimes or always feel their social relationships are not meaningful. In fact, researchers warned that loneliness and social isolation can be as damaging to health as smoking fifteen cigarettes per day.[4] Isolation and lack of community were associated with physical health problems! Even more interesting was learning that friendships reduce the risk of mortality and development of certain diseases. Scientists are even saying that medical care pales in comparison to the powerful positive role that connectedness and social support play in shaping our health.

Yet hiding from each other is so easy, isn't it?

When I was emotionally unhealthy, I rarely let anyone see that. I worked hard on myself in private, waiting until I felt healthy again, and then I talked about the whole process like I was an overcomer, a champion who fought through the fire of the battle and came out the other side. Isolation puts a mask on our face that covers the pain deep inside. It builds walls instead of windows, bringing more darkness than light. It pushes people away instead of drawing them close. Desmond Tutu said, "A person is a person through other persons; you can't be human in isolation; you are human only in relationships."

### We Live in Scarcity

Lastly, most of us live with a scarcity mindset—a deeply held belief in a limited supply of anything—food, water, money, resources, relationships. It's the idea that there will never be enough of __________ (fill in the blank). This mentality leads to unconscious behaviors such as hoarding things from others, competing to stay on top, refusing to share knowledge with others, feeling suspicious of others, avoiding risk, adopting a victim mindset, fearing change, and refusing to help others. Ultimately, if you are living out of fear, you likely are living with a scarcity mindset. Hoarding, suspicion, fear, helplessness, and a glass-half-empty outlook are all opposite of the characteristics we desire in relationships. A scarcity mindset is the opposite of an abundance mindset. Thinking with an abundance mentality helps the village because we want to share with others, collaborate, trust and build rapport, strive to grow together, and believe the best in each other. People who believe in abundance are always generous, even if they don't have much.

My friend Juliet is one of those people. If we hang out and I say, "I love that jacket—it looks great on you!" then somehow, by the end of the night, she has convinced me that the jacket would look better on me and forces me to take the jacket home. She does this every time I visit. I don't know if she just thinks I need some fashion help, but she always finds something to give and graciously tells me, "It will look fabulous on you." She is my reminder that abundance is living life open-handed.

## CREATING THE NEW VILLAGE

The village used to be focused on place—where your family was located in the world. Tribal cultures adapted to their location, dangers, and resources. Yet today the village extends beyond place, family units, and homogenous tribes. In fact, the best villages tend to be intersectional, intergenerational, interracial, with a firm connectivity to self and others. Can you imagine how valuable an inclusive village like this could be? Can you imagine how much you could learn from each other? Maya Angelou said, "In diversity there is beauty and there is strength"—two things we definitely want in our work and for our family.

If you and your partner are going to work, stay in love, and raise a healthy family, it's going to take more than just the two of you. It's going to take a collective of friends who invest together in your family as you in turn invest in theirs. You will need to learn to walk with each other through the fire and the flower fields. You will need to learn how to ask for help and also to give it, and you will need to remember your common ground. But I can't stress this enough: Jeff and I would not have made it to seventeen years of marriage without this village, without our framily. And neither can you.

### More Walking With

I have a patient who had a standing appointment with me every three months for the past eleven years. She has become a dear friend, and I know most aspects of her life beyond treating her for hypertension, diabetes, and obesity. She lives in a food desert, takes care of her younger brother with a mental impairment, and works full-time as a cleaner. Her life is not easy, yet she always wears a bright floral shirt that matches her smile and hugs me tightly at every visit. For years we have been working to help her lose weight to enable her to eliminate some medications for hypertension and diabetes. Her weight has been a lifelong struggle, and financial and environmental difficulties have been a continual deterrent to her health.

One visit she showed up twirling around the room, showing off her impressive weight loss. She had lost twenty pounds! Her blood pressure was finally under control, and her diabetes testing was in perfect range. I proudly thought, "I fixed her!" I praised her hard work and rejoiced with her by shimmying and laughing together. As she left the clinic with her head held high and her smile dazzling, I couldn't help but think, "Yup, I am awesome at what I do" (shoulder brush included).

She returned two weeks later. "That's interesting," I thought. "Why is she back so soon?"

"Uh, what's going on? What happened?"

Gone were the beautiful smile and confidence she exuded two weeks before. Instead she crumbled into the purple chair, sobbing. She recounted the last few weeks: her brother had a medical emergency and was in the hospital, she had been working and then driving directly to the hospital to check on him, she hadn't been able to eat right or exercise, and already she was gaining the weight back. Her blood pressure was high because of the stress, and her blood sugars were increasing due to her poor diet.

"I'm a mess!" she sobbed. "I didn't know who else to talk to, so I just came to see you because I knew you would listen and understand."

As I held her hand in that sterile room listening to her story, I realized I had it all wrong. My job was not to fix her; my job was to *be with her*, to be with her on the journey of life. Some days looked like dancing in those new skinny jeans she could finally wear, and other days it would be sitting in silence sharing tears.

Perhaps you are reading this and remember a time when people abandoned you or forgot to walk with you. Maybe you went through a divorce and half your friends disappeared, disagreed, maybe even judged. Maybe you miscarried your baby and no one knew what to say, so they drifted away. We've all had those times when we feel alone in our sorrows, when we feel like no one would understand. Yet these are the moments when the village is most valuable. This is when we can lean into our community, knowing they might not be able to fix the problems but that they have promised to walk with us no matter what, and that is more than enough. Be the person who leans in. You don't have to be the person who fixes, but always be the person who can sit in silence. When showing up feels awkward and you don't know what to say because sometimes the sorrow is too great, show up anyway. Be ready to sit and hold a hand. Your village is around you; walk with them, sit with them, laugh with them, love them, celebrate with them, cry with them. Hug them. Listen to them. You don't need to have any answers, but you do need to show up.

### More Asking for Help

No one tells you how hard marriage is going to be.
No one tells you that you might not get pregnant.
No one tells you that you might have multiple miscarriages.
No one tells you that your partner might suffer from depression.
No one tells you that you might still feel lonely—even while married.
No one tells you that you might not be happy.
No one tells you that you will grieve differently than your partner.
No one tells you that you might lose your job.

The truth is that no one can tell you all the feelings and experiences you and your partner and family will endure, because your situation is unique. I can tell you right now that life will not unfold exactly as you think or plan. Marriage is so incredibly hard, and my desire is not to gloss over the difficulties that will likely come your way but to be honest that marriage *is* all these difficult things (and more). But here is the truth: love and suffering can be held in the same space.

And you aren't supposed to do the love and suffering with *only* your partner.

Esther Perel says, "Today we turn to one person to provide what an entire village once did . . . Is it any wonder that so many relationships crumble under the weight of it all?"[5]

We can't do life and marriage and parenting alone, yet we won't receive help if we don't ask for help. Why is this the hardest part? I think we all have this same struggle to some degree. I likely have a double master's and a PhD in refusing to ask for help. Besides just stubbornness, we also harbor different fears about asking people for help. Fear of overstepping or imposing, fear of feeling too needy or showing our struggles. These fears hold us back from the gifts of community and force us to carry the burden alone. A wise friend told me that when I didn't ask her for help, I was depriving her of the blessing and delight she found in helping others. Asking for help and helping others is the currency of the village. Stop believing the myth that you can do it all on your own.

Another common myth is that we have to separate ourselves from community to fix our problems before we reengage with those around us. Jeff's dad is a minister, and he says, "It's like clockwork; if a couple stops showing up at church and Bible study groups, it means they are having marital problems." Jeff and I have also noticed this same phenomenon. We've seen countless married couples start to have marital problems and suddenly disappear. They draw inward, struggle through their issues alone, and leave their community of friends. Why do we think that separation can do what only connection can?

We interviewed Roberto and Charlena Ortiz, who shared about the times when Charlena miscarried two of her babies.[6] Charlena was drowning in her despair and didn't know what she needed or how to communicate her sorrow. She talked about a lifesaving moment when her friends stopped by with a "treat yourself" box. It was filled with soothing bath salts, candles, chocolate, and a bottle of wine. She cried remembering the incident. She didn't know what she needed, but that box showed her that she could relax and enjoy a night for herself. She cautions against the phrase "Let me know how I can help," explaining, "This is not helpful! Often when you are lost in sadness, you don't know how to ask for help." But what she and Roberto did do was engage their community in communicating their loss. They told their community they had a miscarriage. They didn't hide; they engaged. Even though they didn't know how to move through their grief or even what they needed in their grief, they shared their worst nightmare with their friends and family. Sharing life with your village leads to greater connection with your spouse.

## More Common Ground

Our friend B.T. Harman uses the unique phrase "partial agreement" in writing about common ground:

> We must allow for partial agreement. We must learn to be in community with those we only partially agree with. We must learn to cooperate with them. We must learn to find common ground around the things on which we do agree. And yes, we even must learn to move forward in friendship. This is the only way to survive—free from isolationist rage—in a diverse world. . . .
>
> Our love must flex.
>
> It must devour the soil of common ground.
>
> It must stretch beyond what our ego is willing to give.
>
> And it must span the cold voids that exist between us. This is the bridging work of love, and I encourage you to begin today.[7]

Common ground is where the collective "we" can thrive and be heard. It means a village with diplomacy. We can all have a voice and make decisions that are good for all, because we have heard each other in a deep and meaningful way. Ultimately, common ground provides a pathway of communication that leads to trust and connectivity. If we see only that we disagree, we will never see the magic that could happen if we found what we agreed upon.

Common ground is also one of the most important facilitators of conflict resolution. In every community we are a part of, there will be conflict; we will disagree with how others parent, vote, eat, and even drive—but these disagreements don't have to ruin the friendship. In fact, these differences often make life much more interesting and colorful. As author Tom Robbins wrote, "Our similarities bring us to a common ground; our differences allow us to be fascinated by each other." Let's choose to live in the wonder and fascination of our village. In doing so, we will see our families and our marriages benefit from the wonder and fascination, the love and respect, the listening and understanding as well.

## HOW TO CREATE THE VILLAGE

**Jeff, do you remember when I decided we were going to start a community garden?**

You mean when I was woken up at 6:30 a.m. on a Saturday by a tractor tearing up half our yard? Yes. I remember it clearly.

**I can't help it if our village showed up to work early and you slept.**

I didn't even know about it!

**Oopsie. Well, that garden was a time when we created a village around a purpose. It was really beautiful. We worked together, shared tools, googled how to grow plants, and ate "farm to table" meals.**

Though I never agreed to this "village plan," it did turn out pretty great. Why did you want to start this thing anyway?

**Well, it stemmed out of a time when we had a group**

**of people we always saw at church but never really saw outside of church. Also, I was looking for excuses to hang out with people more. I needed friends.**

You needed friends.

You may not have a village right now. Maybe you've moved to a new city, maybe you move too much, maybe you just don't know *how* to find your village. I promise that you *can* have a village; one thing and one thing only is needed to do it: intentionality. You will gain no new friends without intention. It will take intentionality to invite someone over for dinner. It will take intentionality to go out of your way to help someone with their kids. It will take intentionality to ask for help. It will take intentionality to pursue others, but we've discovered that when we've intentionally pursued others, we have made deep and lasting friendships. Creating a village looks different for each person and each scenario, but these next principles can help.

### Find the Gaps

Though I started a garden to fulfill my friendship gap, other times we have very practical gaps that can lead to major stress. Where are your tension points between work and love and kids? Where are the gaps where your sanity falls through the cracks? What are those moments that make you feel like you keep banging your head on the table?

I'll give you one of mine: picking up kids from school. One year Jeff and I decided that he would bring the kids to school in the morning and I would pick them up in the afternoon. We both adjusted our work schedules to make this happen. I tried to make it work, but realistically I had no margin at the end of my workday. My last patient visit always ended too close to pickup time, and every day I found myself in a full-on, knees-pumping sprint out the door. Then there were the days my last patient had a medical emergency and I would frantically call Jeff (praying he wasn't in a meeting) so he could help me out of my predicament.

Finally, after the umpteenth time of screaming my frustrations in the car while running late for pickup, I had the Oprah "aha moment" that I could change this! I could find a way to close this gap and give myself a reprieve. So I did. That night I confessed to Jeff my struggle with the current arrangement, and the sweet, kind prince of a man he is asked the most loving question: "What can I do to help?" Just hearing that question made me sigh in relief. We made changes to our schedules (again), and the gap was closed. The tension released.

Your partner is part of your village. Be honest about the tensions you face. What are your repeated head-banging moments? What are the gaps?

Are you constantly fighting with your partner about your house being a mess?
*Village win:* Hire cleaners! You don't have to do it all. You can think of it as a luxury or an absolute necessity.

Do you find that you have no spare hours to yourself?
*Village win:* Ask a high school kid to come over after school to play with your kids for two hours so you can have a few moments to breathe (or hide in your room with the door locked).

Are you constantly fighting with one kid over math homework, causing meltdowns and crying fits?
*Village win:* Find a math whiz (who isn't you) who can tutor your kid.

Do you feel like you are always so serious and need more fun in your life?
*Village win:* Find a friend who is fun, and hang out with them more!

What about ways *you* could love your village? It's not just about closing your gaps, but helping close others' gaps as well.

What about when you have delicious leftovers from dinner that won't be good the next day?
*Village win:* Text your neighbor and take the food to them.

What about when you're about to leave town and have extra perishables in your home?
*Village win:* Call your neighbor and show up with a surprise gift basket.

What about when the big game your village enjoys is going to be on?
*Village win:* Invite them over, and say it's comfy clothes only.

What about when you're heading to the park to play with the kids?
*Village win:* Text a friend and pick up their kids along the way, giving them an hour of reprieve.

Some things cost money; some things don't. You can get as creative as you want. You can also decide to sacrifice some finances to bring you some sanity! The key is to take inventory and determine what is worth changing so you can work, stay in love, and raise a healthy family.

**Build Your Squad**

You can have all the friends in the world, but if you are in a committed relationship or marriage, it is important that the people in your village are *for* your relationship. Their support encourages relational health and longevity. If you are just starting your marriage or committed partnership and all your friends are still single and want to keep dragging you to the clubs and living the single life, I guarantee their continued involvement in your life will cause friction between you and your partner. You don't need to drop all your single friends, but you do need to make sure the friends you surround yourself with are for your relationship and respect that commitment.

Jeff always says, "Who you listen to will define who you become, and the way your community is diversified will define you." In the words of motivational speaker Jim Rohn, "You are the average of the five people you spend the most time with."

So surround yourself wisely. Who are your five people? Do you admire them? Are they positive and uplifting? Are they real and honest? Are they people who think like you, or do they make you think more? Are they in the same stage of life, or are they older—so you can learn from them—or younger—so you can pass along wisdom?

I'm not asking you to be selfish and handpick your village so everything benefits you. No, the diversity of your community will not allow for that. You will have hard times, you will butt heads, you will not like each other some days, you will roll your eyes at certain antics, but overall, you will know that the people who surround you make you better and you are in it with each other for the long haul. For better or for worse.

**Jeff, this reminds me of all the times you decide to go to bed whenever you want, even if we have a huge gathering of people at our house!**

Listen, if I'm tired and I'm in my own house, I should not feel bad about going to bed. Everyone knows this about me. I go to bed early. I'm also awake early.

**I also think you are just done with people.**

Also true. I can be extroverted with people up to a certain point, then I need some alone time.

**I think it's funny that no one cares anymore—they know this is just you. Grandpa Jeff is going to bed early, like usual.**

Hey, we all have our differences. Don't hate.

One question I frequently ask myself is, do I feel safe only within the village of sameness? This is a gut check question to make sure I'm not getting too comfortable and cozy only with people just like me. Sameness is comfortable, but it's also boring. This question is my reminder of the importance of radical inclusivity. A reminder of the dignity and honor due to all people, especially those who are not like me. A reminder to reach out to the margins, beyond my comfy bubble, and sit and listen and learn. A squad with differing voices may be uncomfortable but is definitely not boring. As a bonus, you will gain a broader worldview and a greater understanding of humanity.

### Create Community

**Ten years ago we started a thing called "Shinabrunch."**

It started because we had a small group of work friends who were very wealthy and we didn't know what to give them for Christmas. So instead of gifts, we invited them to our home and cooked a monstrous brunch for them on New Year's Day.

**I think it started with about ten people. We didn't have kids**

**at the time, but we invited their whole families. They drove their fancy cars to our little house in the city. We hung out all day eating, playing with kids, and watching football.**

Then they all moved away and we realized we needed new friends. We wanted to continue our New Year's Day tradition.

**We had been going to a church and knew a few people there, so we decided to invite them. We told people to come in their pajamas. We ate, played games, took naps, and watched the New Year's Day parade.**

That year we had a whole new group of friends show up. The following year we met new friends at work, so we invited them too.

**And somehow we kept inviting more and more people. Any new person we had met that year was added to the list.**

Ten years later, we have over one hundred people come through our house for Shinabrunch.

**It's the best day of the year.**

I think it has taught us that our village has shifted and changed a lot with different phases of life. And that's okay too.

**We adjust and adapt as friends move, people change, and life throws all its curveballs.**

Yet it has always taken intentionality to send the text with the Shinabrunch invite to all our friends and hope that people will show up.

We are not alone in this journey of work, love, and parenting. We don't have to be alone, and we probably won't make it if we try to do it alone. Something will have to give. We can intentionally let go of our individualism, scarcity, and isolation and instead resolve to walk vulnerably with each other as we find common ground. We can appreciate and embrace a village that is diverse, that is supportive of our marriages, and that teaches our kids. We can both work and, dare I say, change the world with a support squad. We can stay in love when we stay connected to our community. And our children will become the sum of the collective love of our village.

In the next chapter, we want to imagine your future family. Not your family of origin, not your current family, but the family you hope to become.

## TALK ABOUT IT

Before you move forward, take a moment to answer these questions on your own and invite your partner to discuss them with you.

1. Who are the people in your life who make it all possible? Have you stopped to thank them for how they contribute to your village?
2. Where is there a gap, and who do you know who could help with that need? Call them and ask for help.
3. Is there someone you need to hire or swap services with who can help you feel less exhausted? Why haven't you done it yet, and how can you make it possible?
4. Is there someone in your village with whom you need to share something you are struggling with? Or is someone suffering or struggling who may need you? Call that person today, and invite them into your pain or walk with them in theirs.

## DO A CHALLENGE

We all need creative ideas for taking what we read and putting it into practice. Share your experience with others and tag @loveorwork #loveorwork.

***Get help with one thing.*** We know that the majority of you reading this book are exhausted and need some help. So pick just one thing and ask for help. It might be hiring a cleaner one time or maybe asking a friend to babysit for a couple of hours to give you some margin. Or what if you chose this one week to use a grocery delivery service to save you time? Choose one thing to allow you to get a breath of fresh air, and check that one thing off your never-ending to-do list.

## LISTEN UP

Add to this journey by listening to a free podcast that relates to this chapter and will give you even more to process. Go to www.loveorwork.com/listenup.

### Preemptive Love: Jessica and Jeremy Courtney (Episode 32)

If you are interested in learning more about the village mentality, we recommend you listen to a podcast interview we hosted with two incredible leaders: Jessica and Jeremy Courtney. They are the cofounders of a nonprofit organization called Preemptive Love, and Jeremy is the author of the book *Love Anyway*.

Families that stay together are willing to give up something for the sake of each other.

-Jeff Shinabarger-
#LOVEorWORK

CHAPTER 12

# *Labor of Love*

## JEFF

**The future depends on what we do in the present.**

—MAHATMA GANDHI

For better or for worse. In sickness and in health. Right, André?

**What is it with men and the endless whining when they are sick?**

What is it with you not believing me when I am sick? Remember the pepperoni pizza incident?

**How could I forget? The one time I didn't believe you were sick.**

It was the holiday season and we were decorating cookies. All of a sudden, my gut started grumbling. So I told you I didn't feel well.

**And I told you it was probably just a little gas. Let's be honest: it wouldn't be the first time.**

I decided I would take a shower and see if I felt better. Suddenly, it was all coming up. I whipped open the shower curtain to lean over the toilet.

**Stop. You did not make it to the toilet in any way, shape, or form. I walked into the bathroom to find my grown husband naked with his hands on his knees, water running over his head, and pepperoni pizza sprayed across the entire bathroom. Every. Single. Wall.**

Whoa, whoa, whoa. I am not the bad guy in this story. I told you I was sick.

**Did you have to projectile vomit like a five-year-old?**

Well, that's a good point.

**I cleaned you up, dried you off, and helped you get into bed.**

You were so sweet. You got me snuggled in all nice and cozy.

**Yes, and then I heard a whimper from the bedroom.**

"André?"

**I came running in. "What's wrong?" And how did you answer?**

I said something like, "André . . . can you clean up the bathroom? The smell is kind of making me gag."

**I was like, he did not just ask me to clean up that pepperoni bathroom too! I wanted to run out the front door. But I decided to stay. For better or for worse, in sickness and in health . . . in cleaning up pepperoni puke.**

We get the opportunity to create what family looks like in regard to love and work. This is where we wipe the slate clean from our family of origin, from societal norms, from past mistakes, even from current mistakes and decide we want to chart our own path moving forward. Maybe certain parts of this book have been impactful and you hope to include those ideas or principles in your family, or maybe not—you get to choose. This is your unique story. This is your meaningful work. This is the love of your life. You get to choose to stay in love.

While we were developing this project, doing our research, and writing this book, people often asked us for advice. We love their interest and their questions, but we still struggle to answer. We understand the tension between love and work as much as anyone else and continue to peel back new layers every day. How do you end a book about a topic that is not complete? There is no final chapter that can sum up all the answers for real people wrestling through a complicated topic.

Just when you think you have it figured out, you encounter a plot twist. I was reminded of this truth when we talked with Ben and Liz Forkin Bohannon, cofounders of Sseko Designs, a fair-trade clothing and jewelry company bringing work and education opportunities to women in Uganda.[1] They have two small kids and both work hard to lead this organization. They shared with us a story about when they felt like they were in a good rhythm in life. By the time their firstborn son was a toddler, they had figured out childcare, what time they would get to work, and what time they would leave. They had a good plan balancing work and travel. They were killing it. *Until they weren't.* It happened one day when their son got sick and messed up their perfect plans. They looked at each other and expected the other person would take care of him. They both had important meetings that day.

They both had their own plans. Everything had to come to a screeching halt.

We think we have it all worked out—until we don't.

That is the exact point of this entire book. None of us are experts. Even when you implement all the suggestions from this book, there will be days that go sideways. Plot twists that poke holes in our perfect plans. The tension of love and work doesn't get easier with time (or writing a book)—it just compounds. But that doesn't mean we quit. It means there is more work and love we need to keep wrestling through.

Along this journey we have found a few guiding principles to rally around. Maybe these will encourage and inspire you as you figure out your own family strategy going forward.

## WE WORK TOWARD EQUALITY

I am in this together with André; I am not in charge of her. I give up individual rights and she gives up individual rights for us to be in partnership collaboratively. The age of a male-dominant home has officially left the equation. Are there times she asks me to make a decision? Yes. And there are many times I ask her to make decisions for our family. You see, if we are both going to pursue our meaningful work, we both have to value each other's decision-making. When we choose to partner with someone for life, we are willing to give up some things. Equality in regard to time, purpose, responsibilities, sex, chores, and power is respected and encouraged.

The value we place on equality in our home is setting a new precedent for our children and their children. A common statement we heard throughout our interviews was, "I want my daughter to believe that she can be and do anything she wants to be and do. I want my son to see that all women can and should pursue their purpose in life and work. And I am trying to be an example to them." We agree!

*Love and work is possible when we believe we are better together than we are on our own.*



## WE WORK TO STAY

More than half of the families from my generation have been impacted by divorce, which is one reason couples today are questioning if marriage is a smart option for their relationship. More people are choosing not to marry or are entering into marriage later than ever before, and the divorce rate in the last twenty years has slowly declined.[2] A new study published in the *Journal of Marriage and Family* says that one explanation for the decline in marriage is a short supply of economically stable partners.[3] Today, people are much more pragmatic about marriage. Even with major shifts in why or when people get married, every couple has their own reasons for wanting to stay together. We think one reason couples stay together and connected is their belief that they are better together than they are on their own.

When we first got married, I hoped the few little things I disliked about André would change and she'd become the perfect wife I always imagined. In the last eighteen years of our marriage, I have been married to about three different versions of André, and the same is true about me. Our relationship has spurred continual self-reflection. Do I contribute as much as I receive? Do I passionately pursue her for connection, romance, and friendship? Is her life better with me in it? Is it my turn to stay home with the sick kid?

I can't say this enough—I am a better human because André is in my life, and I know she would say the same thing about me. We have a long-term view. No matter how many times we mess up the questions of balance and priorities, we will always apologize and choose each other again and again. We are willing to work on ourselves, willing to work at life together, and willing to work to stay, even when we don't feel like it.

*Love and Work is possible when we are willing to give up something for the sake of the other.*

## WE WORK TO CHOOSE LOVE

The *American Journal of Society* reports that working couples are married 14 percent longer than single breadwinner families, and our research showed that working couples believe they are better parents because of their work. Separation at work gives us more things to talk about when we come together. Time apart can be good for togetherness. The problem is that we choose work over love more often than we care to admit. We don't mean to do it. It starts innocently. We schedule a conference call in the evening. We respond to a message in the bathroom. We come home thirty minutes later than we planned. It's the little choices that quickly become the normal way of life. Work at home. Work all the time. Work now takes priority over everything.

I've learned that I have to do a check-in every couple of weeks. How many times did I choose work before my family? Usually more than I want. I feel a persistent battle within me to keep doing my work when what I need to do is continue being in love. I wish it got easier with time, but it actually seems to get harder with progress in our culture. You see, as technology has integrated everything in life, it has blurred the lines of love and work. My phone keeps bringing my work home. I decided to write a letter to my phone. We needed to break up.

> Dear iPhone,
>
> I remember meeting you for the first time and thinking you would make my life so much easier. I thought I needed you to do what I do better. Now I can't seem to get away from

you. You cause me constant concern and a physical separation from people I love most. The more I am away from you, the more human I feel. Touching you makes me feel out of touch with myself and others. You can't solve what I want, what I need, or who I am. You are not the solution to my need; you are just one way I can share my needs. Do you hear me now? You may give me access, but you also make me anxious. There are many times that you add fun to my life, help me capture special memories, and make distance go away. So here's the deal: I don't want you to impact my attitude or my attention or my friendships anymore. I think we need to set some boundaries. I like you, but I don't love you. I am ready to make a change. Hey, Siri, I think we need some space.

The first time I created separation from my phone, it created a healthy separation from my work and a healthy reminder of who I love. When was the last time you said goodbye to your work or technology and chose to prioritize your love? Families that stay together are willing to give up something for the sake of each other. Maybe this little phone check-in should be an indicator of who we love.

*Love and Work is possible when we choose family over everything.*

## WE WORK TOWARD PURPOSE

Have you ever been to a silent disco? You walk into the room and everyone in the room is dancing, but you hear nothing. Hence the name. It's an all-out dance party with no music. Everyone is wearing wireless headphones. Multiple channels of music are being broadcast to the headphones, and each person gets to choose which channel they listen and dance to. It's not uncommon for people to be singing at the top of their lungs to their song, forgetting they have headphones on. As you look around the room, headphones lit up in red, green, or blue indicate that the dancers are boogying to three different songs. Sometimes the DJ will sync them all together so one song plays on all the channels and everyone dances together, but most of the time the room is a hodgepodge of dancing, singing, and grooving to different musical styles. A great example of the tension of love and work is a silent disco where everyone has chosen a different channel. We all want to listen to our own music, but if we always choose our own song, we will never dance together.

Isn't it true that life is like a silent disco where we're dancing to our own beats? As a human, I want the freedom to pursue my purpose. As a husband, I want André to feel the freedom to dance to her own song. And as a father of two children, I want to help each of them find their unique purpose and fuel their passions with everything I have been given. Yet everyone in a family can easily isolate themselves with their own tune, unless we craft intentional moments to make our music match so we can dance to the same song together.

We have to plan moments of intentionality to bring everyone together. Sometimes that means we all focus on one purpose as the priority for the family in a certain season. Sometimes we organize schedules to make everyone's work possible. Sometimes one person pays bills so another person can live their dream. But at some point we all have to turn on the same song and dance in unison.

*Love and Work is possible when we prioritize each person's individual giftings.*

## IS IT POSSIBLE TO CHANGE THE WORLD, STAY IN LOVE, AND RAISE A HEALTHY FAMILY?

For three years we have been wrestling with this question: Is it possible to change the world, stay in love, and raise a healthy family? We have asked people around the country—while touring in an Airstream, over the phone, in video conference calls, through in-person interviews, and over dinners. We attended events, used social media and even analyzed the findings of a formal nationwide survey. After all this work, what is the answer to this simple question? First of all, the question is not simple; it's complicated. We started this project because we feel this tension every day in our own lives and the lives of people we love. We needed this project as much for us as for you. Now it's time to give you our answer. Is it possible?

What do you think, André?

**I think it is possible. And I believe it's worth pursuing. There is always a possibility of failure, but anything worth pursuing involves risk. So if you want to have it all, then go for it. But go for it with wisdom, guidance, and tools in your tool belt to navigate the difficult roads that are bound to come your way. This pursuit will not be easy and will not happen on its own. You will need much intentionality and effort.**

**I also don't want to overprioritize changing the world. I don't want people to think that "changing the world" is the goal in life. "Changing the world" can look very ordinary. In our celebrity culture, it's hard to remember the importance of the ordinary. The importance of the people without the check mark on social media. Life-changing work is done every day that people don't see on social media, and it matters. World-changing things like teaching kindergarteners how to read, babysitting for your friends, extending kindness to those on the streets, cleaning up trash in the neighborhood. Who decides that these beautiful acts of service aren't world changing? I would argue that it all matters.**

Staying in love while changing the world may look like many different things depending on each partner's purpose. And if you're like me and Jeff, you're bound to have great differences in purpose, but that is where the adventure begins. The wonderful thing about love is that it is always an outward flow: toward our partner and toward this messed-up world. Love looks for the good of all who are concerned, and it always includes the good and the bad. This energetic flow of love toward each other and the world is precious and rare; it is a gift to behold and is worth pursuing with all our heart.

Raising a healthy family while staying in love and changing the world may be the hardest part of all, but again, I've seen it working in the lives of hundreds of couples we interviewed. Every family is different, so there is no "one way." Holding both the tension and the fight for this pursuit is extremely valuable. For me it starts with "letting go" to a Higher Power because my humanness cannot do it all alone. My limited, selfish, control-seeking ways will never accomplish this goal. So I believe in a Higher Power that works in all and through all and will walk with all of us along this journey to our destination, together in love.

There you have it. My last two cents. What about you? What do you think, Mr. Shinabarger?

I think it is 100 percent possible. And at times it feels 100 percent impossible. But I believe this combination is how life was intended to be. We were made to work, to love, and to raise little humans who work and love. I want to do everything I can to experience all those elements in my own life and desire the same for you. When I live this way, I feel fully alive. When I do what I'm made to do, the world will get better. When you and I stay connected, both our lives are better. When I'm investing in my kids, I believe future generations will be better. I want the days that we live to have a purpose beyond our time on earth. I hope after I leave, there are imprints left behind, not only through work projects but more so through our children.

Throughout this project I've seen how all three intertwining realms are character building. I know I am better with you. I am more fulfilled when I am doing meaningful work. I am deeply grounded and humbled when raising my children. These three aspects of life are building me into a better man, a better version of myself.

I can't deny this project has impacted me spiritually as well. When I do meaningful work, I feel a deep sense of spiritual connection to a Being who is greater than me. For me, when it's working, it seems like God is working through me for others.

**But are there times you doubt you can do it all?**

I absolutely have doubts every day. I have fears along the way, and some days I want to give up. It is hard to do any of these elements on their own and even more challenging when you combine them. Nobody said being married would be easy. Nobody said raising good humans would be easy. And nobody said changing the world would be easy. But everyone would say all these things are extremely worthy pursuits. And they are much more rewarding collectively than individually. I wouldn't choose any other way.

**That reminds me of driving to Disney World.**

If you read our introduction, we shared how we started this whole project with an Airstream adventure. This book would not be complete if we didn't tell you the rest of the story—a story we dubbed #Americandreamfailure.

**It all started with good intentions and a vision for "the American dream."**

Here's the epic idea: we would pick up the kids early from school and take the Airstream to Disney World and combine it with an awesome *Love or Work* podcast interview with the founders of Rifle Paper Company. We would do it all! Combine all three together: our work, time together as a couple, and a family adventure.

**And the best part is that the kids had no idea what was ahead. We would keep it from them until we rolled through the Disney gates while the kids screamed with delight! We'd capture their surprise on video and post it on Instagram. (Hello, best parents ever!)**

So off we drove to Florida. The kids were in the back seat asking hundreds of questions about where we were going, while we laughed and dodged their incessant questioning, when about four hours into driving, something went terribly wrong.

**It felt very similar to our VW moment, when suddenly the truck slowed to twenty-five miles per hour in the middle of the highway. I know what you're thinking. "André, you really need to get ahold of this whole running out of gas problem." Not this time, friends! It was not my fault!**

That's right, for the first time, it was not because you ran out of gas. This time there was something very wrong with the truck hauling our Airstream. We pulled off the highway at the next exit to "the middle of nowhere" south Georgia.

**Listen, there is the South, and then there is the deep South, which is a whole different category.**

We frustratedly pulled into the only auto shop we had seen in the last five miles and prayed someone would be able to help us out while Neko shouted from his booster seat, "Hey, guys, it's okay! It's not an adventure until something goes wrong!" (Thanks for the reminder, kid.)

**Then a man with a wad of chew, a cigarette hanging out of his mouth, and only four teeth stepped out of the shop, and my hope plummeted.**

He really did only have four teeth. I held on to hope and explained the truck situation to the man, and honest to God, I could hardly understand him. I mean, I'm sure he was speaking English, but wow, his southern accent was something else. As he stuck his head under the hood of the truck, I did pick up one phrase: "Aw hell, these new trucks. You know they got them damn computers . . ." It wasn't looking good.

**Needless to say, he did not know how to fix a truck with a computer, so we called the nearest dealer. It was a Friday evening, and no one could look at the truck until the next day. Then who knew how long it would take to fix the problem?**

And one more problem: the Airstream could not stay at the dealer while the truck was being fixed.

**Yeah, big problems. But the biggest problem of all?**

Jada piping up from the back seat, "Mom, Dad, are we still going to our special surprise?"

**To say we were in a cluster of a situation is to put it mildly.**

Here's a quick rundown of how it all went down: Found a nearby trailer park where we could park the Airstream (for who knew how long). Canceled the podcast interview in Florida (so disappointing). Dropped the truck off at the dealer the next day. Rented a car and drove home.

**But none of those details mattered as much as the moment during dinner at the restaurant—the only sit-down restaurant in the miniscule town.**

Yup, we were eating pizza and had to break it to the kids that we had planned to go to Disney but wouldn't be able to go. André and I were defeated and heartbroken.

**With tears in my eyes, I made the great confession. "Kids, we are so sorry. We were going to take you to Disney World, but now we can't go." I awaited the tears and emotional breakdown of my kids with bated breath.**

They looked at us and looked at each other, shrugged, and then said, "That's okay. So do you think we could go back to the Airstream and have a movie night together?"

**"Wait. What? That's it? You just want to watch a movie?"**

And then the kids said, "We don't want to go to bed."

That night we all squeezed together on the Airstream bed in the middle of nowhere, while a thunderstorm raged around us, and cozily snuggled in to watch a movie together.

The great vision of our American Dream trip did not come to fruition, and neither did the work interview, but ultimately, we were together and that was enough. Love was enough.

## THE ONLY ANSWER THAT MATTERS

When we started this journey, we asked if it was possible to do all three: change the world, stay in love, and raise a family. But the question we learned along the way that might be more important is how? How do we maintain it all? How will you and your partner find meaningful work? How will you prioritize and pursue each other to stay in love? And how will you raise good humans who will grow up and change the world? Your way will not be the same as our way. There will be days when everything is clicking and you feel a sense of wonder. These are the days to celebrate and be grateful. There will be other days when it feels like everything will most certainly fall apart. These are the days to have grace with yourself and with each other, then reset your expectations and edit the logistics. You get the opportunity to write the story that works for your family. You get to create a love story that is vulnerable, romantic, and world changing. You have the privilege of making this grand idea work in your home, in your work, and with your favorite person. You are in charge of creating the mantra for a better way forward.

The greatest assurance we have found to date is a shift in our perspective. The question is not only *if* we will find the balance between love and work but also *how* we will do love and work together. And through our research, questions, and crazy stories, we hope we have given you some direction toward a better way. Yes, it is possible to change the world, stay in love, and raise a healthy family. Now it's your turn to make love and work possible.

**LOVE OR WORK.**
May our love story grow.
May we see our limitations.
May we struggle through the tensions.
May we find meaningful work.
May we love our partner's purpose.
May we create a new normal.
May we choose each other first.
May we stay on the same team.

May we find time to rest.
May we be vulnerable physically and emotionally.
May we raise good humans.
May we ask for help when we need it.
May we create a better future, together.
**LOVE AND WORK.**

# Acknowledgments

Thank you to the village that has written this story. We have never done this alone.

Thanks to all the moms and all the dads (or those desiring to be moms and dads) attempting to do this everywhere (especially ours): Dan and Judy Shinabarger and Don and Sandy TenHoeve: your love has been the greatest example to us.

Thank you to the team: Kayla (and Joseph) Stagnaro, your lives have helped shape this concept all along the way (Kayla, this project would not be in existence without your care and commitment). Lydia (and Andrew) Mays, these words would be lost without your voice, your encouragement, and our cozy writing days together. Our agent, Christopher Ferebee, thanks for believing in our ideas. Brooke Hempell and the Barna Group, thanks for giving data to our dream. Woody Faulk, thanks for believing in sustaining marriages and giving to this project right from the start. Matt (and Amena) Owen, you have listened to every podcast and made us sound better all along the way. Ali Nelson, thank you for always bringing beauty to our work. Thank you to each person who has made this project better. Bethaney and Alex Wilkinson, Tuere and Nate Butler, Caroline White, Michaella Till, Ben Farnham, Chantel Adams, Blaine Williamson, Haley Solomon, Mary Claire Stewart, Campfire Social, Ale Trevino,

McClaine Wellem, Zac Holben, The Sandoval Team, Kevin Jennings Jr., Kevin Jennings Sr.

Thank you to the team at Zondervan: Mick Silva, Kim Tanner, Tom Dean, Andrea Kelly.

Thank you to the early believers in this project: Brittany and Andy Thoms, Andy Levine, The Airstream Marketing Team, See Spark Go, Heather and Andy Trilling, Ponce City Market, Jamie and Molly Hargather, Jeff and Alycea Hylton, Bryan and Shannon Miles, Seth and Renee McLaughlin, Rob Bell (and everyone at our retreat when we shared this crazy idea).

Thank you to our framily: Chris and Teri Bledsoe, Katie and Josh Thompson, Jim and Allison Dudley, Jimmy and Mandy Starnes, Anne Curtis, Tammy Huizenga, Amanda Hightower, Anne Seymour, Kerry and Roger Brockwell, Cathy Price, Kathryn Taylor, Nathan and Whitni Freeman, Jonathan and Callie Rich, Scottie and Natalia Parker, Kyle and Juliet Korver. Working through the good and hard parts of life with you all has given us hope and a drive to keep going.

Thank you to our sisters and "the outlaws": Mike and Karyl Morin, Beth and Jon Gaus, Joanna and Matt DeWolf, Megin and Mike Stearns, and all our nieces and nephews (we can't wait to meet all your future families). Raising families together is one of the greatest joys. You have taught us so much.

Thank you to all the people we have learned from on our podcast and at dinners having the hard coversations: Dana and Angelo Spinola, Liz and Ben Bohannon, Kitti and Bill Murray, Shannon and Jeremy Cowart, Keri and Brian Fosse, Cecilia and Terence Lester, Dorcas Cheng-Tozun, Mary Stuart and Joel Iverson, Connie and Frank Sabo, Erin and Josh Guerrieri, Ashley and Kyle Jones, Jennie and Zac Allen, Katherine and Jay Wolf, Donna and Leroy Barber, Vik and Scott Harrison, Gregg and Jeff Foxworthy, Brett and BT Harman, Danica and Jason Russell, Ashley and Collin McHugh, Stacy and Ken Coleman, Hannah and Tripp Crosby, Sarah and Steve Dubbeldam, Kaitie and Jared Bryant, Nikolle and Jose Reyes, Laurel and Peter Greer, Becca and Steve Dziedzic, Laurie Watson, Lecrae and Darragh Moore, Sam and Toni Collier, Mama Z and Dr. Z, Phileena and Chris Heuertz, Jennifer and Mike Foster, Laura and Ben Harrison, Martavia and Jarius Wynn, Taylor Levy and Che-Wei Wang, Joy and Billy Phenix, Shauna and Aaron Niequist, Tori and Dr. Henry Cloud, Charlena and Roberto Ortiz, Beverly and Todd Sandel, Glen "Beleaf" and Yvette Henry, Rebekah and Gabe Lyons, Tina and Frank Fernandez, Lyndie and Chris Carneal, Amanda Van Dalen, Chelsea Sabo, Jeanne and Jarrett Stevens, Jess and Jake Ekstrom, Emily and Chris Norton, CC and Tristen Sutton, Hillary and Jason DeMeo, Jessie Artigue and Gerard Brown, Brooke and Christian Hempell, Jessica and Joe Honegger, Susan and Josh Robinson, Necole and Chris Marlow, Brielle and Jeremy Slate, Stacie Brinkman and Øivind Loe, Allison and Jim Dudley, Jennifer and Kyle Sapaugh, Joanna and Nolan Waterfall, Brad and Kristi Montague, Matt and Margaret Reynolds, Danielle and Tedashii Anderson, Brett and Christine Kirouac, Daryl and Cathy Heald, Amy and Kohl Crecelius, Greg and Lisa Gilbert, Eryn Eddy, Drew and Natalie French, Erin Bernhardt, Sarah Buchanan-Sasson.

Thanks to our early readers and the people who have made the work better along the way: Andy and Cristina Mineo, Rick and Lynn Mercer, Nicole and Alan Chang, Beth and John Jarrett, April and Rodney Stammel, Brett and Aynsley Younker, Nicole and Khalil Thompson, Gisele Lempola, Andrea Proctor, David and Mallory Farmer, Stephen Lewis, Aaron Fortner, Andrew and Kim Case, Shantel Kriss, Monica and Michael Lage, Joe and Talia Bunting, Sela Missirian, and Hayley and Kramer Johnson.

Lastly, to our Plywood People community: we are thankful to walk in this tension with you. We hope our imperfect and crazy stories become conversation starters for your relationships and lead you to deeper connections with the people you love.

# *Notes*

## Chapter 1: The Great Adventure

1. https://www.enneagraminstitute.com/
2. Tim Ferriss, "The Tim Ferriss Show Transcripts: Arianna Huffington (#274)," February 2, 2018, https://tim.blog/2018/02/02/the-tim-ferriss-show-transcripts-arianna-huffington/.
3. Brené Brown, *The Gifts of Imperfection: Let Go of Who You Think You're Supposed to Be and Embrace Who You Are* (Center City, MN: Hazelden, 2010), 18.
4. Ali is our dear friend and the amazing artist who designed the quotes throughout the book. Check her out at @alimakesthings.

## Chapter 2: Pick One

1. Dana and Angelo Spinola are the founders of Fab'rik. Check out their women's clothing and Asher collection: www.fabrikstyle.com.
2. Listen to *Love or Work* podcast episode 1 with Dana and Angelo Spinola: https://podcasts.apple.com/us/podcast/day-dating-sabbaticals-and-fashion-angelo-dana-spinola/id1409843661?i=1000415497224.
3. Scott and Vik Harrison are the founders of Charity: Water. Learn more about their work at www.charitywater.org.
4. Listen to *Love or Work* podcast episode 23 with Vik and Scott Harrison: https://podcasts.apple.com/us/podcast/charity-water-vik-scott-harrison/id1409843661?i=1000425928223.
5. https://www.thegivingkeys.com/

6. Katrina Trinko, "Gen Z Is the Loneliest Generation, and It's Not Just Because of Social Media," *USA Today* (May 3, 2018), https://www.usatoday.com/story/opinion/2018/05/03/gen-z-loneliest-generation-social-media-personal-interactions-column/574701002/.
7. Founders of Gravity. Learn more about their work at https://gravitycenter.com.
8. Listen to *Love or Work* podcast episode 45 with Chris and Phileena Heuertz: https://podcasts.apple.com/us/podcast/enneagram-and-choosing-no-kids-phileena-chris-heuertz/id1409843661?i=1000439423486.

## Chapter 4: Three Love Stories

1. Amy Elisa Jackson, "We Just Can't Unplug: 2 in 3 Employees Report Working While on Vacation," Glassdoor (May 24, 2017), https://www.glassdoor.com/blog/vacation-realities-2017/.
2. Hector Garcia, *Ikigai: The Japanese Secret to a Long and Happy Life* (New York: Penguin Random House, 2016), 10.
3. Laura and Ben Harrison are the founders of a social enterprise that provides modern eyewear for children. Check out their business at https://jonaspauleyewear.com.
4. Listen to *Love or Work* podcast episode 47 with Ben and Laura Harrison: https://podcasts.apple.com/us/podcast/running-start-up-while-parenting-differently-abled/id1409843661?i=1000441022145.
5. The story of Skylar Jones has inspired a group of selfless photographers. See how their work is providing hopeful memories in times of grief: https://lovenotlost.org.
6. Listen to *Love or Work* podcast episode 13 with Ashley and Kyle Jones: https://podcasts.apple.com/us/podcast/grief-in-marriage-ashley-kyle-jones/id1409843661?i=1000421311040.
7. If you ever have a chance to travel through Atlanta, please take time to visit a coffee truck that is bringing together a refugee community: www.refugecoffeeco.com.
8. Listen to *Love or Work* podcast episode 4 with Bill and Kitti Murray: https://podcasts.apple.com/us/podcast/intimacy-parenting-boys-and-cancer-bill-kitti-murray/id1409843661?i=1000417702546.

## Chapter 5: Seasons of Purpose

1. Alex Erdekian, "It's Time to Reevaluate the Powderpuff Tradition," Wayland Student Press (November 25, 2013), https://waylandstudentpress.com/39635/articles/its-time-to-reevaluate-the-powderpuff-tradition/.
2. Listen to *Love or Work* podcast episode 34 with Hannah and Tripp Crosby: https://podcasts.apple.com/us/podcast/mental-health-living-without-secrets-tripp-hannah-joiner/id1409843661?i=1000431506119.
3. Listen to *Love or Work* podcast episode 25 with Gregg and Jeff Foxworthy: https://podcasts.apple.com/us/podcast/marriage-is-funny-gregg-jeff-foxworthy/id1409843661?i=1000427147111.
4. Listen to *Love or Work* podcast episode 18 with Juliet and Kyle Korver: https://podcasts.apple.com/us/podcast/nba-little-kids-and-road-trips-juliet-kyle-korver/id1409843661?i=1000423655218.

## Chapter 6: Same Team

1. "Gottman Card Decks" app, Gottman Institute, https://www.gottman.com/couples/apps/.
2. The Known Project sells flip books of questions that inspire conversations for marriage or friendships: www.knownproject.com/products/.
3. Listen to *Love or Work* podcast episode 37 with Katie and Jared Bryant: https://podcasts.apple.com/us/podcast/the-known-project-kaitie-jared-bryant/id1409843661?i=1000433884213.
4. If you are looking for something to spice up conversations with your partner, check out Defy Drift Cards: https://defydrift.com.
5. Terry Gaspard, "Timing Is Everything When It Comes to Marriage Counseling," Gottman Institute (July 23, 2015), https://www.gottman.com/blog/timing-is-everything-when-it-comes-to-marriage-counseling/.
6. Tedashii is an incredible hip-hop artist. To listen and learn about his music, visit http://reachrecords.com/artists/tedashii/.
7. Listen to *Love or Work* podcast episode 16 with Danielle and Tedashii: https://podcasts.apple.com/us/podcast/dinner-conversation-tedashii-danielle-anderson-matt/id1409843661?i=1000422758697.

8. Listen to *Love or Work* podcast episode 35 with Steve and Sarah Dubbeldam: https://podcasts.apple.com/us/podcast/the-creative-process-steve-sarah-dubbeldam/id1409843661?i=1000432137973.
9. See the exhilarating experiences and inspiring magazine named *Wilderness*: https://wildernesscollective.com.
10. Read the inspirational articles and campaign from Darling Media: https://darlingmagazine.org.
11. Listen to *Love or Work* podcast episode 51 with Joy and Billy Phenix: https://podcasts.apple.com/us/podcast/between-parents-joy-billy-phenix/id1409843661?i=1000443898601.
12. Listen to *Love or Work* podcast episode 65 with Jeanne and Jarrett Stevens: https://podcasts.apple.com/us/podcast/productivity-and-intimacy-jeanne-jarrett-stevens/id1409843661?i=1000453393983.
13. Fred Rogers, *The World According to Mister Rogers: Important Things to Remember* (Boston: Hachette Books, 2003), Kindle edition.

## Chapter 7: Care and Capacity

1. Parker J. Palmer, *Let Your Life Speak: Listening for the Voice of Vocation* (San Francisco: Jossey-Bass, 2000), 61.
2. Alan Shelton, *Transforming Burnout: A Simple Guide to Self-Renewal* (Tacoma, WA: Vibrant, 2006).
3. Palmer, *Let Your Life Speak*, 96.
4. Listen to *Love or Work* podcast episode 19 with Jay and Katherine Wolf: https://podcasts.apple.com/us/podcast/hope-heals-katherine-jay-wolf/id1409843661?i=1000424118762.
5. Check out www.hopeheals.com to read more of Jay and Katherine Wolf's story and buy their newest book, *Suffer Strong: How to Survive Anything by Redefining Everything* (Grand Rapids: Zondervan, 2020).
6. Richard Rohr, *The Universal Christ: How a Forgotten Reality Can Change Everything We See, Hope For, and Believe* (New York: Convergent Books, 2019), 83.
7. Capacity definition. New Oxford American Dictionary.
8. David Whyte, *The Three Marriages: Reimagining Work, Self, and Relationship* (New York: Penguin, 2009), 287.
9. *Traveling Unfamiliar Pathways* (Denver: Renovaré, 2013), 51.
10. This was modeled after an exercise in Helen Cepero's book

*Journaling as a Spiritual Practice: Encountering God through Attentive Writing* (Downers Grove, IL: InterVarsity Press, 2008).

## Chapter 8: Get Away

1. "Time Off and Vacation Usage," U.S. Travel Association, https://www.ustravel.org/toolkit/time-and-vacation-usage.
2. Alexander E. M. Hess, "On Holiday: Countries with the Most Vacation Days," *USA Today* (June 8, 2013), https://www.usatoday.com/story/money/business/2013/06/08/countries-most-vacation-days/2400193/.
3. Listen to *Love or Work* podcast episode 38 with Nikolle and Jose Reyes: https://podcasts.apple.com/us/podcast/working-together-side-by-side-nikolle-jose-reyes/id1409843661?i=1000434392162.
4. Karen Rayn, "Take Vacations to Heart," July 16, 2007, *Los Angeles Times*, https://www.latimes.com/archives/la-xpm-2007-jul-16-he-vacation16-story.html.
5. Lolly Daskal, "Four Scientific Reasons Vacations Are Good for Your Health," Inc., June 13, 2016, https://www.inc.com/lolly-daskal/4-scientific-reasons-why-vacation-is-awesome-for-you.html.
6. "Good Guys," *This American Life*, January 10, 2014, https://www.thisamericanlife.org/515/good-guys.

## Chapter 9: Sex Talk

1. Lawrence B. Finer, "Trends in Premarital Sex in the United States, 1954–2003," *Public Health Reports* 122 (January–February 2007): 73–78.
2. Yella Hewings-Martin, "The Female Orgasm: What Do Women Want?" *Medical News Today* (October 6, 2017), https://www.medicalnewstoday.com/articles/319671.php.
3. World Health Organization, "Defining Sexual Health," 2006, updated 2010, who.int/reproductivehealth (retrieved April 22, 2020).
4. John Gottman, Julie Schwartz Gottman, Doug Abrams, and Rachel Carlton Abrams, *Eight Dates: Essential Conversations for a Lifetime of Love* (New York: Workman, 2018), 100.
5. Brené Brown, *Daring Greatly: How the Courage to Be Vulnerable Transforms the Way We Live, Love, Parent, and Lead* (New York: Penguin Random House, 2012), 2.

6. Emily Nagoski, *Come as You Are* (New York: Simon & Schuster Paperbacks, 2015).
7. Listen to our *Love or Work* podcast episode 42 with Laurie Watson: https://love-or-work.simplecast.com/episodes/the-sex-talk-laurie-watson.
8. Listen to our *Love or Work* podcast episode 83 with Cristina and Andy Mineo: https://podcasts.apple.com/us/podcast/love-or-work/id1409843661?i=1000465798522.
9. Keith Leavitt, "Maintaining an Active Sex Life May Lead to Improved Job Satisfaction, Engagement at Work," March 6, 2017, Oregon State University, https://today.oregonstate.edu/archives/2017/mar/maintaining-active-sex-life-may-lead-improved-job-satisfaction-engagement-work.

## Chapter 10: Raising Humans

1. Kristi Walker, Kristen Bialik, and Patrick van Kessel, "Strong Men, Caring Women: How Americans Describe What Society Values (and Doesn't) in Each Gender," Pew Research Institute (July 24, 2018), https://www.pewsocialtrends.org/interactives/strong-men-caring-women/.
2. Stephanie Pappas, "APA Issues First-Ever Guidelines for Practice with Men and Boys," *Monitor on Psychology* 50, no. 1 (2019): 34, https://www.apa.org/monitor/2019/01/ce-corner.
3. Tresa Undem and Ann Wang, "The State of Gender Equality for U.S. Adolescents," Plan International (2018), https://www.planusa.org/docs/state-of-gender-equality-summary-2018.pdf.
4. Daniel Goleman, *Emotional Intelligence: Why It Can Matter More Than IQ* (New York: Bantam Dell, 1998), 189.
5. To read more about masculine role norms, check out Ryon C. McDermott et al., "In Search of Positive Masculine Role Norms: Testing the Positive Psychology Positive Masculinity Paradigm," *Psychology of Men and Masculinity* 20, no. 1 (April 2018):12–22.
6. Hillary McBride, "Undoing the Shame of Our Body Image Struggles," *For the Love* podcast with Jen Hatmaker, season 14, episode 3, http://jenhatmaker.com/good-change-episode-03-hillary-mcbride.htm.
7. Check out Lindsay Kite's TEDx Talk, "Body Positivity or Body

Obsession? Learning to See More and Be More," at https://www.youtube.com/watch?v=uDowwh0EU4w.

8. To read more about body neutrality, see Anuschka Rees, *Beyond Beautiful: A Practical Guide to Being Happy, Confident, and You in a Looks-Obsessed World* (Berkeley, CA: Ten Speed, 2019).
9. Tara Mohr, "Why Women Criticize Each Other—Plus Ways to Play Bigger," https://goop.com/work/career/why-women-criticize-each-other-plus-ways-to-play-bigger/.
10. Keli Finnerty-Myers, "Are You Medial Literate?" *Darling*, October 22, 2014, https://darlingmagazine.org/are-you-media-literate/.
11. Ann Voskamp (@annvoskamp), "Being joyful isn't what makes you grateful … being grateful is what makes you joyful," Twitter, October 9, 2014, https://mobile.twitter.com/AnnVoskamp/status/520359318084804608.
12. Brené Brown, *Daring Greatly: How the Courage to Be Vulnerable Transforms the Way We Live, Love, Parent, and Lead* (London: Penguin, 2013), 125.
13. "Leadership and Parenting, Part 1," *Andy Stanley Leadership* podcast, https://podcasts.apple.com/tt/podcast/leadership-and-parenting-part-1/id290055666?i=1000428959400.

## Chapter 11: It Takes a Village

1. Listen to *Love or Work* podcast episode 20 with Chris and Teri Bledsoe: https://podcasts.apple.com/us/podcast/philosophy-strategy-tactics-for-life-family-chris-teri/id1409843661?i=1000424547902.
2. Sebastian Junger, *Tribe: On Homecoming and Belonging* (New York: Hachette, 2016), 18, Kindle edition.
3. "Address of His Holiness Pope Francis to the Participants in the Conference Organized by the Dicastery for Promoting Integral Human Development" (April 4, 2017), http://w2.vatican.va/content/francesco/en/speeches/2017/april/documents/papa-francesco_20170404_convegno-populorum-progressio.html.
4. "The 'Loneliness Epidemic,'" Health Resources and Services Administration (last reviewed January 2019), https://www.hrsa.gov/enews/past-issues/2019/january-17/loneliness-epidemic.
5. Esther Perel, *Mating in Captivity: Reconciling the Erotic and the Domestic* (New York: HarperCollins, 2006), 13, Kindle edition.

6. Listen to *Love or Work* podcast episode 55 with Charlena and Roberto Ortiz: https://podcasts.apple.com/us/podcast/grit-virtue-charlena-roberto-ortiz/id1409843661?i=1000446143284.
7. B.T. Harman, "The 54321*," Countdown No. 035.

## Chapter 12: Labor of Love

1. Check out Ben and Liz Forkin Bohannon's amazing work at www.ssekodesigns.com.
2. Jay L. Zagorsky, "Why Are Fewer People Getting Married?" June 1, 2016, The Conversation, https://theconversation.com/why-are-fewer-people-getting-married-60301.
3. Daniel T. Lichter, Joseph P. Price, and Jeffrey M. Swigert, "Mismatches in the Marriage Market," *Journal of Marriage and Family* (September 2019), https://doi.org/10.1111/jomf.12603.

**LOVE**
*or*
**WORK**

is a project of Plywood People.

Plywood is a nonprofit in Atlanta leading a community of start-ups doing good.

To learn more, visit Plywoodpeople.com.

PLYWOOD

# LOVE *or* WORK

THE PODCAST!

It doesn't have to be over yet! You can tune in to the *Love or Work* podcast to learn more from couples who are doing the work. Many of the couples mentioned in the book were featured on the podcast.

If you want to learn more, subscribe - wherever you listen!

LoveorWork.com/Podcast